THE ODYSSEY YEARS

A Novel View of the Vietnam Experience

D1248397

By Mike Konz

Contents

INTRODUCTION

ODYSSEY - a long wandering usually marked by many changes of fortune.

My decade long journey began soon after I escaped the confines of High School, a source of much anxiety for me. Algebra, Geometry and Chemistry – when numbers and letters started getting mixed together - were particularly baffling. My only relief came in History and in English Literature classes. Sometimes history, literature and myth come together in a great adventure story. My favorites were THE ILIAD and THE ODYSSEY by the Greek poet Homer. They tell the tale of the great Bronze Age warriors Achilles; Hektor, the Trojan; Ajax; and the cunning last hero standing, Odysseus.

By the summer of 1965 the brewing struggle between the Communist North and Democratic South Vietnam and the involvement of the United States in this matter entered into the consciousness of the American people. Soon many had choices to make. Mine would lead to meeting the incarnated spirits of those ancient warriors.

Matt Kelly, 1975

BOOK I

WHAT WAS I THINKING?

CHAPTER I

The Road Less Traveled

In every venture, the bold man comes off best.
Athena, *THE ODYSSEY*

"I, Matthew Kelly, do solemnly swear that I will support and defend the constitution of the United States against all enemies, foreign and domestic; that I will bear true faith and allegiance to the same; and that I will obey the orders of the President of the United States and the orders of the officers appointed over me, according to the regulations and the Uniform Code of Military Justice. So help me God."

This sounds serious. I guess there is no backing out now – but what have I gotten myself into? I started out to go to college. I'm not sure why, but that's what all of my friends were doing. Some might ask "If your friends were jumping off a bridge would you do that too?" For some of us, the answer is "Yes".

How I got into college in the first place is a mystery to everyone, especially my high school guidance counselor. I guess a minor talent, in a minor sport, lacrosse, yes "nerd hockey", helped. By mid 1st semester, in the Fall of 1964, it was obvious that the things which plagued me in high school; laziness, lack of focus, were no better in college. I would go into math or science class determined to learn the day's lesson. For the first five minutes I would listen intently. Then, unfortunately, my focus would switch to many other and wondrous things. Forty five minutes later, I didn't have a clue. But the first five minutes I had down pat. I did much better in English Literature and History but it was doubtful that I would make it to lacrosse season.

"Things were a changin'." Words from a folk song by Bob Dylan or maybe Peter, Paul & Mary. Clearly that held true for me. By the end of the semester my grade point average indicated I was not going to be successful as a college student. Since there was a prohibition against playing lacrosse and not attending classes, I dropped out.

Many things were in evolution. Folk music was popular on college campuses and in the coffee houses of the major cities, particularly New York. The coffee houses were patronized by those known as Beatniks. Most Beatniks would have gone to high school in the 1950s. To me they seemed like an odd group who wore sunglasses at night, berets and goatees (the guys, not the girls). I preferred "Doo Wop" - the city street corner sound. I was also a closet country and western fan; at night alone in my room, not in ear shot of friends, I would listen to Hank Williams and Patsy Kline on my record player. All of this was being moved aside by the California surfer noise of the Beach Boys, and the music of a new group from England called The Beatles. The tone of folk music was becoming more integrated into the civil rights move-ment, and more aware of the conflict in Vietnam – which President Johnson said he would keep us out of. Drugs, especially marijuana, were slowly moving from the urban coffee houses onto college campuses and the "square" world of suburban America. Even the "Beat Gener-ation" was losing ground to a new, undefined social movement The "Beat" icons like the writer Jack Kerouac and the poet Allen Ginsberg were beginning to fade in the light of a growing "psychedelic" phe-nomenon lead by a Harvard professor, Dr. Timothy Leary. His exper-imentation with the "mind expanding" drug LSD now held the key to enlightenment.

After I dropped out of college, I went to work for a small, local house framing contractor. Our job was to build the plywood deck, the 2x4 walls, door frames, the roof etc. - the skeleton of the house on top of the foundation. The lead carpenter needed skills to read the blueprints; a vision to see the finished product; and good math skills, especially geometry, to understand how to cut the lumber at the proper angles so that all the framework would fit together. After viewing my manual skills for a couple of days the lead carpenter, realizing I would be a menace around the circular saw and power tools in general, relegated me to carrying the wood studs and other lumber from place to place where the more skilled crew members could make use of them. In addition to carrying heavy things, I was not bad at hammering nails. It was clear, however, that I was not going to become a skilled carpenter.

By the time we graduated from high school, many of my classmates had busted through the fog that envelopes most teen aged brains. My lacrosse teammate, and friend, Allen Richmond is a prime example of this. From the time we were in 5th grade Allen wanted to be an International Lawyer. Neither of us knew exactly what that entailed, but his course was set. At that time, I still wanted to be a fireman or a cowboy. Allen was accepted at the University of Pennsylvania and many of my friends populated the top schools in the east: Penn State, Rutgers and Colgate to name a few. Now it was two years after graduation and I still wandered around aimlessly without intent or purpose.

I began to research another option, the military. The armed forces have equivalent occupations of most civilian jobs. Everything from engineering, truck driving, mechanics, typists, you name it, and some branch of the service has it. In fact, only one out of twelve service people become combat troops. Everyone else is in a support position. Naturally, as Robert Frost's poem about the road not taken suggests, "I took the road less traveled" and decided to be the one in twelve. We will see if that makes "all the difference". The only choice left, which branch? The Air Force, unless you were a pilot, or had mechanical skills, seemed rather mundane. The Navy, I could not see myself spending that much time at sea and I did not like the uniforms. That left only the Marines and Army. With apologies to John Wayne in "The Sands of Iwo Gima", storming the beaches from landing craft still involved too much time on ships at sea. The Army it is! The Army Airborne to be more precise. Now I have gone from one out of twelve to one out of one hundred. Jumping out of planes surely was a road less traveled.

❖   ❖   ❖

The wily Odysseus left his island kingdom of Ithaca; the king, Agamemnon, and his brother, Menelaus, - husband of Helen – departed from Sparta, who's city had no walls; and the immortal Achilles, The Commander of Myrmidons, from parts unknown in Greece. All sailed the treacherous Aegean Sea to meet before the fabled citadel of Troy.

I, without legacy or reputation, would begin my military sojourn from somewhat less legendary Newark, New Jersey by bus in the middle of the night. How many great adventures begin in this fashion is undocumented. But there we were, about forty bewildered recruits; some draftees, but mostly volunteers, heading for Fort Dix training center in the heart of the New Jersey Pine Barrens. Apparently, I wasn't the only one with a focus problem.

I did not find basic training particularly difficult. I was in pretty good shape so the running, marching and physical training were not very challenging. Some of the classroom stuff, like map and compass reading I enjoyed. For a suburban boy I turned out to be a decent marksman at the rifle range. However, the Drill Instructor's obsession with making beds (hospital corners, bouncing quarters off the tightened blankets) was annoying. In other words, I was not very good at that.

Training Companies consisted of about 160 recruits with 4 platoons of about 40 men with a Drill Instructor who was a Sergeant, of various rankings, in charge of each platoon. An officer or two was lurking about but we rarely saw them. Each Platoon had an acting Platoon Leader and four Acting Squad Leaders all of whom were trainees themselves. Prisons have a similar system. Whenever there are not enough Guards to cover all responsibilities, some control is ceded to the inmates themselves. Those inmates who have gained the confidence of the Guards are delegated as "Trustees" and assigned responsibilities. How our "Trustees" were picked, I did not know.

This is how an Army Training Company is broken down: four Squads in each Platoon, and two Fire Teams in each Squad. My Acting Squad Leader was Jack Cucina. It turned out he was a couple years ahead of me in the same college and also from a neighboring town. We had mutual friends both at school and home. One day Jack and I plus two other recruits were called out of our Company morning formation to meet with the Commanding Officer (C.O.). He asked us if we were interested in going to Officer's Candidate School (OCS) after Basic Training. Jack accepted, I don't remember what the others did, but I declined. It was a good move for Jack, a little older and a lot more mature than me. I wasn't sure where this great adventure was heading, and I wasn't ready for any other responsibilities.

In training soldiers learn the difference between Sergeants, who are Non Commissioned Officers (NCOs), and Commissioned Officers: Lieutenants, Captains, Majors and such. Officers are saluted and called "Sir" by enlisted men. They receive their commission by an act of Congress. Most Officers come from military colleges or universities such as West Point, Virginia Military Institute, and The Citadel. Many other colleges have a Reserve Officer Training Corps (ROTC) program on campus. Enlisted men can become officers, if qualified, by completing a three month program at Fort Benning, Georgia.

I think of the Officers as the executives of a corporation, the "Suits". The Sergeants (NCOs) are the foremen. Among the responsibilities of NCOs are; training, small unit operations and, most importantly, keeping young, inexperienced 2nd Lieutenants from getting into too much trouble in combat. Sergeants are not saluted or called "Sir".

During training, many a rattled recruit with a Sergeant Drill Instructor in their face shouting incomprehensible orders, has blurted out a resounding "Yes Sir!" to appease their antagonist. To their dismay, they are then greeted with an expletive laced rebuke of "Don't call me sir!. I'm not an Officer. I work for a living."

Only one event jumps to my mind about Basic Training. We had rooms, not the communal rows of bunks you see in movies, with eight men to a room. My roommate Bill was a college graduate and a High School teacher in the Boston area. A gentle soul, but not in very good shape. He had much difficulty with the rigors of P.T. One evening while quick marching (not exactly running, but close to it in cadence march) back from the rifle range Bill was falling behind.

The Drill Instructors (D.I.s) often made those falling off the pace run double time around the marching platoon. I never could understand the logic to this. Bill fell victim to this punishment and soon was in obvious distress. He could not continue. Jack took charge and got the DI to allow Jack and me to carry Bill, in the Fireman Carry

Technique we had learned, back to the barracks. The rest of the group continued as usual.

I do not think the D. I., nor Jack and I realized how serious Bill's condition was. When we got back to the barracks Bill was rushed to the Base Hospital. We were told late that night that Bill had died from cardiac arrest. No one from the Platoon was asked any questions about the incident. The D. I. in charge of the Platoon was replaced.

The training continued as if nothing had happened. The Trainee Platoon Leader, Private Chuck Harper, had been in the Army before. Discharged, he went to work at a civilian job for a few years and decided he liked army life better. However, he had to repeat basic training. His prior service was the reason for his appointment to Trainee Platoon Leader. Harper seemed determined to keep a lid on talk about the incident. Bill's death was the first encounter I had with the death of a young man. I wondered how much more of this I would witness. Although I'm not sure how Bill's death should have been handled, something about it all put me ill at ease.

Our trainee leader thought I didn't take training seriously enough. That was true for the first five or six weeks. Bill's death, however, gave me a sobering outlook with regard to what we were doing for the last few weeks. Basic training was complete. I would be going to Fort Gordon in Georgia for Advanced Infantry Training. Others in my class would be going to other posts throughout the country, depending on their job assignments, for additional training.

Cucina was going to Officers Candidate School at Fort Benning in Georgia. Over the last eight weeks he had proven himself to be a natural leader. The other recruits looked to him for advice and guidance. He, however, had to deliver to me the bad news that I was not recommended by Private Harper for promotion from Private E-1, the lowest pay grade, to Private E-2. I was pissed. I had finished in the top tier of our training class in all categories.

When our official orders and Certificate of Training Completion were issued, I was surprised and pleased to see that Harper's lack of recommendation was overlooked, and I made it to Private E-2.

I arrived at Fort Gordon in early February of 1966 expecting the "sunny" south to be much warmer than New Jersey. True there was no snow on the ground, but the weather was surprisingly cold. Our barracks were not the modern, college dorm-like facilities I had gotten used to at Fort Dix. They resembled the World War II era wooden barracks that housed the entire training platoon and was kept somewhat heated by a coal fired stove. We took turns standing nightly watch over the fire to make sure it didn't run out of fuel.

Our new Company Commander, at our first reveille formation, let us know that our entire company was comprised of Airborne volunteers and that we would go on to jump school together, then most of us would be assigned to parachute units in Vietnam. I knew, of course, the path I had taken would eventually lead to Vietnam. But hearing this stark statement added a chilling touch of reality.

Our days were filled with physical training, small weapons instruction including the M-60 machine gun and M-79 grenade launcher, fire and maneuver, and escape and evasion tactics. We also learned the nineteen standing orders issued by Major Robert Rogers to his Rangers during the French and Indian War in 1759. Among my favorites are #4 "Tell the truth about what you see and what you do. There is an army depending on us for correct information. You can lie all you please when you tell other folks about the Rangers, but don't never lie to a Ranger or Officer", and #5 "Don't never take a chance you don't have to." I vowed to obey all nineteen orders, and especially #5.

We kept out of trouble and were busy most days and nights. We did, however, have more time off than in basic. I, along with others, made several visits to the near by town of Augusta. This may be a great place for the Masters Golf Tournament (we didn't get to see the course), but not very welcoming for a bunch of lowly army recruits. But the beer was cold and no one asked for I.D.

It was during one of these sojourns to town that, after a couple of cold beers, I made some disparaging remarks about our new trainee Platoon Leader. Private First Class (E-3) Waters played favorites. He liked to be kissed up to and if you did you generally got better treatment; more time off, easier extra details for example. He constantly curried favor with the D.I.s but I'm not sure if it helped him. The D.I.s seemed pretty focused on their mission. His brown nosing did annoy many in the platoon, me included. My words got back to him. In response, he tried to make my remaining time a living hell.

Every morning at reveille formation the D.I. would ask the leaders of each Platoon for a couple of men for special details – generally not fun ones. While the details were usually spread out among everyone, I was called on all of the time. It got to the point that I didn't wait for Waters to call my name. I just ran out of formation to where the D.I.s assigned the tasks. This amused the Platoon and the D.I.s, but not so much PFC Waters. Creating this frustration for Waters helped to lighten my load.

One evening in the barracks after a day of training Waters began chewing out the whole platoon for making him look bad in front of the D. I.s. Exactly what our transgression entailed, I do not remember, but the louder he got, the more the platoon began to chuckle and smirk. I saw my opening and remarked, "Hey Waters, are you losing control?" He immediately jumped in my face and challenged me to a fight, I quickly accepted. The time, one hour after mess hall. The place, behind the barracks. I showed. He didn't. His reign of terror over me ended that night.

By late March, 1966 we completed Infantry Training. As a Company we packed our duffel bags and bounded onto four buses to traverse the state of Georgia from east to west from Augusta to Columbus. A very uncomfortable, six hour journey through the night. Occasionally I would drift off to semi-consciousness, only to be jarred back to semi-awareness by sudden turns and bumps on the back roads of Georgia. Somewhere in the darkness between dusk and dawn we arrived at Fort Benning.

The Black Hats greeted us. Parachute Training Instructors were fully in command here. Their black baseball caps distinguished them from us. There would be no trainee platoon leaders. PFC Waters was just another face under a helmet. He no longer had any power over anyone's actions.

The sole focus here was to prepare us for jumping. Opportunities to punish or volunteer for extra duties stayed behind at Fort Gordon. From sunup until sundown, the training was intense and rigorous. We ran constantly. We practiced jumping from a height of one foot off the ground to learn our parachute landing fall (PLF). We jumped from a mock-up of an airplane door about thirty feet off the ground to practice our jumping form. Attached to a cable, we slid down about one hundred feet from the mock door. We jumped from a two hundred and fifty foot tower that resembled a ride you would see at Coney Island. Then came the medieval torture device, the "suspended harness". Thirty or forty trainees strapped into parachute harnesses just hanging from the roof of an open sided shed, rectangular in shape with a boardwalk on the perimeter where the Black Hats would patrol. I'm sure they were giving us some verbal instructions, but as the harness straps that were wrapped around our thighs slowly began to shift, and squeeze our crotches, the pain blocked out all other senses. I was on the outside of my row, next to the boardwalk. I managed to shift my foot ever so slightly to be able to just touch the platform enough to relieve some of the pressure of my body pushing down from the harness and ease the pain. Obviously I wasn't the first hapless trainee to attempt this. As a Black Hat quickly discovered my cheating. Without saying a word, he grabbed the riser (the part of the harness above my shoulders), and shook it vigorously. This instantly added to my pain and discomfort. As I winced in agony, the instructor smiled and moved on like the bad guys in Western movies. I now knew why they wore black hats.

Three weeks of Jump School at Fort Benning went by quickly. The training was strict and prepared us well for our first jump. Most trainees had flown in planes before but there were several local boys who had not. We had to complete five successful jumps to earn our wings. After taking off and jumping out of a plane five times, I wondered how those guys were going to handle landing in a plane for the first time.

The main event came, our first jump. In the early morning we lined up in our sticks alphabetically. The Army does not do anything at random. The C-130 Hercules carried us on our short flight to the drop zone. Fort Benning spills over the Chattahoochee River into Alabama and that was our target. I for one could not believe we were actually going to jump out of this perfectly good airplane. What I believed didn't matter. What mattered was what the Jump Master thought and he thought it was a good day to jump. The Jump Master began a series of commands, shouts and hand gestures we had heard and seen ad nauseum over the past three weeks:

1.   Get Ready
2.   Inboard Personnel Stand Up
3.   Outboard Personnel Stand Up
4.   Hook Up
5.   Check Static Line
6.   Check Equipment
7.   Sound Off Equipment Check
8.   Stand In The Door – the final and scariest of them all

I was thankful I wasn't the first in the stick.

The cadence we sang on our P.T. runs took on a more relevant meaning:

Stand up – Hook up – Shuffle to the door
Jump right out and count to four
If that chute don't open wide
You'll be a dot on the mountainside

I prayed there were no mountains in southern Alabama. I took off my glasses and placed them in my breast pocket. Feigning blindness to break the tension, I asked the Trooper in front of me, Ed Kane, if he would let me know if my chute opened when we jumped. He grinned, and assured me that he would. The fateful moment came. The Jump Master yelling, "Go! Go! Go!..." as each Trooper moved to the roar of the open door. Out we went.

The din and clamor of the C-130 was suddenly replaced with a stunning silence. We could hear each others' yells of exhilaration. I couldn't resist, I yelled to Kane, who was several yards below me and to my left, "Hey Ed, is my chute open?" I could hear the smile in his voice when he replied, "Oh yeah Kelly, its open." For the remaining few seconds I concentrated on my landing - "Keep your eyes on the horizon as you approach the landing. Knees and feet together. When you feel your toes touch the ground – Hit – Shift – and Rotate." The mantra the D.I.s drilled into us paid off.

I made what I considered to be a perfect landing. I couldn't wait for the next four jumps to earn my wings. On our second and third jumps, I again shouted to Ed "Is my chute open?" By the third jump, the usually soft spoken southerner yelled back, "Kelly, you dumb ass, if it didn't, I'd be shouting down to you and not up!" I got the point. My humor had lost its charm. But Ed's response had me grinning all the way down.

Airborne Training complete, we were sent on leave for about two weeks. We reassembled at Fort Benning and boarded a Pan American 707 bound for Saigon. We all had orders as replacements for airborne units, we just didn't know which ones; the 101st Airborne Division, 173rd Airborne Brigade or the 1st Airborne Brigade of the 1st Cavalry Division.

There we were, 150-200 newly minted and bewildered para-troopers and five very skittish stewardesses. They served us our meals, laughed at our lame jokes, and clearly had a great deal of sympathy for our fate. It all had the appearance of an exotic group vacation. I don't think our fathers went off to World War II in such style.

My Dad and Uncles sailed to Europe on troop ships known as Liberty Ships, slightly longer and wider than a football field. They were crammed on with about eight thousand others, sleeping below deck like sardines in hammocks. Our journey took fifteen hours, while their's lasted seven to ten days and did not include any sympathetic steward-esses. We suffered an occasional bout of air turbulence. Their vessels were subject to attack by German U Boats by which many were torpe-doed and sank.

It was midday when we landed at Tan Son Nhat Airport in Sai-gon. As we exited the plane, we all gasped in turn. The scorching heat sucked the oxygen from our lungs and the humidity was so thick, you could almost sip the moisture from the air. As we formed up on the tarmac, sweat poured off us from every possible outlet and from some places I didn't know I had.

An Officer welcomed us to Vietnam and informed us that we would spend about three days at a staging center to allow time for us to acclimate to the weather and other special conditions. During that time, we would also be assigned to our respective units. I did not think three days would be enough. A fleet of buses appeared, and off we went.

CHAPTER II

Rules of Survival

Many cities of men he saw and learned their minds, many
pains he suffered, heartsick on the open seas, fighting to
save his life and bring his comrades home.

Homer, *THE ODYSSEY*

Our three days of orientation and acclimation were up. I, along
with about thirty others, was assigned to the 1st Airborne Brigade of the 1st Cavalry Division stationed in the central Highlands of Vietnam. We were loaded in a Chinook helicopter. My first
of many helicopter rides. The Chinook is powered by tandem rotor
blades, one at each end of the aircraft. It can carry up to 7,000 pounds.
It is the work horse of the 1st Cavalry. In addition to transporting
troops in the interior regions, it was also used to move artillery pieces
and heavy supplies by strapping harnesses to the underside of the fuse-
lage. Equipment would dangle about fifteen feet below the Chinook.
This proved to be an advantageous method for delivering fire power to
the top of a mountain. From the outside, at least to me, it resembled a

cross between a grasshopper and a preying mantis.

The trip was about two to three hours long and uneventful. I would occasionally look out the small portal near my seat and see nothing but miles of lush green trees. Of course I imagined a Viet Cong behind every tree drawing a bead on our aircraft with his AK-47. The NCO in charge let us know we were approaching Camp Radcliff. We all rushed to the windows and strained our necks to get a glimpse of our new home. On top of a prominent hill, we saw a large painted emblem of the 1ˢᵗ Cavalry. It resembles a shield from the middle ages, rounded at the top and tapering to a blunted point at the bottom. The shield is yellow in color with a wide black stripe at a diagonal across the shield and the head of a horse in the upper left. From what we could see, the base itself resembled a Civil War encampment with acres of large, olive drab tents. This was not at all like the barracks of our training days.

The heart and soul of any army is the Infantry. Paratroopers are included in this group, although we resent being lumped in with the regular ground pounders. Tanks, Artillery, Transportation, Aircraft etc. are all there to support the "Queen of Battle", the Infantry. The Queen is the most versatile piece on a chess board, so too must the infantry be the most versatile on the battlefield.

The building block of an American Combat Division like the 1ˢᵗ Cavalry is the Fire Team - generally 5 soldiers led by a Sergeant (E-5 is the pay grade). Two Fire Teams make up a squad led by a Staff Sergeant (E-6). Four Squads make up a Platoon led by a Second Lieutenant, with a Sergeant First Class (E-7), as second in command. Four Platoons make up a Company led by a Captain with a small Headquarters staff with a 1ˢᵗ Lieutenant as the Executive Officer, the First Sergeant (E-8) referred to as "Top" (as in the top non-commissioned officer in the Company). Sometimes he is called something less flattering depending on the mood of the troops. A Medic, and a few clerks round out the H.Q. Staff. Four Companies make up a Battalion led by a Lieutenant Colonel, with a larger staff consisting of several officers plus a Sergeant Major (E-9) as an assistant. Four Battalions make up a Brigade led by a Full Colonel plus more staff. Three Brigades make up a Division commanded by a Major General. All in all, about 15,000 Troops, counting support units, are in a Division. A Corps may have as many as five Divisions commanded by a Lieutenant General. I still don't understand how a Major outranks a Lieutenant, but a Lieutenant General outranks a Major General.

I suspect, as in the case with my new Company, most military units throughout history were undermanned. New Recruits are at a premium as death, disease, and injuries happen faster than replacements can be found. This caused less experienced enlisted men to fill in as squad and team leaders when a Sergeant was not available to take on the job. This made our transition to our new home a lot easier since we were looked at as men who could share the load and not as interlopers trying to break into a clique. Of course there was some mild hazing, and us newbies got to carry any extra paraphernalia needed on a mission; machine gun ammo, claymore mines, C-4 explosives, etc.

Along with seven other new arrivals, including Ed Kane, Bob Palmer and Andy Browne from my jump school class, we were assigned to the reconnaissance platoon of Company D of the 1st Airborne Brigade of the 1st Cavalry.

The platoon was headed by Lieutenant Heffner, a recent graduate from the Reserve Officer Training Corps at Ohio State. The real leader, however, was Staff Sergeant Roy Maxwell. Maxwell was skeletal in stature, slightly over six feet tall and weighing about one hundred fifty pounds, with deeply etched lines in his weathered face which gave him the appearance of someone much older that his thirty nine years. Maxwell never said where he was from and never talked about his life prior to the military. If asked where he came from, he would reply "I used to come from The Corps, but now I am from the Airborne." His frequent use of the colloquialism "y'awl", and his accent suggested southern roots. Never one to stand on formality, he said "You can call me sergeant if you want, but I prefer 'sarge' or 'Max', whichever suits you." Max did not need the affectations of rank. He knew and the troops knew who was in charge. Max reminded me of a French Foreign Legionnaire. Legionnaires came from many different countries, probably many had an unsavory, mysterious or questionable past. As long as they took an oath swearing loyalty to The Legion, not to France, and they made it through training they were accepted with no questions asked. Max, like all of us, took the oath to the Constitution but his loyalty had a higher calling; to his "Airborne Legion". The facts we did know were that he joined the Marines in late 1944 and saw limited action in the

Pacific at the end of World War II. Max was with the 1st Marine Division in 1950 at the outbreak of the Korean War. Again, a war between a communist North and a democratic South. The North Koreans launched an attack on the South. The United Nations supported the South. Under the command of General Douglas MacArthur, American and U. N. forces eventually pushed the North Koreans back to the Yalu River which marked the border of Communist China. The Chinese amassed about 120,000 soldiers at the border, crossed the Yalu River, and surprised the 1st Marine and several Army Divisions at the Chosin Reservoir, soon to be known as the "Frozen Chosin" as the temperature fell as low as -40 degrees during the seventeen day battle that started on November 17, 1950. The Marines, outnumbered approximately eight to one, inflicted heavy casualties on the Chinese, but were forced to withdraw. Major General Oliver Smith, the commander of the 1st Marines said, "Retreat Hell! We're not retreating, we're just advancing in a different direction." Max was part of that experience, and we would benefit from his knowledge and insights on survival. Luckily there was not much of a chance of the temperature dropping to -40 degrees.

Max told us he spent time in the Marine Corp Jail. Sarge was a Drill Instructor at Parris Island, the Marine Boot Camp, in the late '50's when Congress began to investigate abuse of recruits by D.I.s. A Congressman looking into charges at the training base was questioning Max's recruits. He asked one if the Sergeant had ever hit him. The recruit responded "Yes sir." We all know Marines do not lie. When asked why, the recruit said it was because he could not shoot straight. "Well can you shoot straight now son?" interjected Max enthusiastically. The reply was a resounding "Yes Sir!" This fact didn't help Max, who went to the brig anyway. Eventually he was released and found a home with the Airborne. Paratroopers know a good soldier when we see one.

Max was not known for his smile but on occasion, when amused, he grinned wryly. Trying to keep us rookies alive during those first few months gave him plenty of reason to grin. The first month of a combat tour, in the opinion of the platoon's experienced veterans is the most dangerous. Rookies tend to be surprisingly less cautious. Top offenses are; freezing upright like a deer in the headlights when shooting started, the proper position is your head and ass as low to the ground as possible; lack of awareness of the danger that surrounds a soldier in the field

RULES OF SURVIVAL // 25

from pit viper snakes, land mines, pungi pits and other aptly named booby traps such as hand grenades rigged to a trip wire across a trail.

There is the tale of a new replacement, Private Betz, from the hills of West Virginia who announced to the company on the day he arrived his intention of winning the Congressional Medal of Honor. The veterans quickly labeled him a casualty waiting to happen and kept their distance. As predicted, within two weeks while returning from a patrol with his squad he was not paying attention and tripped a hand grenade booby trap. The problem is, the booby trap was set around his platoon's defense perimeter. Betz carelessly strayed out of file formation as the squad returned from patrol. The patrol leader yelled at him to stop, but too late. Betz was seriously wounded, not life threatening. Luckily no one else took a hit from the flying shrapnel. Betz returned home with a Purple Heart Medal, clearly not his goal.

Max really didn't have much to say either way about us being in Vietnam. He would say, "I'm an American soldier, so I'd fight the Canadians if sent there. Just don't feed me a bunch of crap about how evil the Canucks are." He always referred to the Army of the Republic of Vietnam (ARVN) as our valiant, freedom loving, South Vietnamese Allies fighting off the Godless Communists from the North. His unique outlook gave us much to grin about too.

Oddly enough, in spite of his cynicism, he would remark on the Berlin Airlift and the Berlin Wall: "It seems to me people were trying to break out of East Berlin and not into it. The communist revolutions in Cuba caused hundreds of thousands of people to flee. What fate awaits these poor dumb Vietnamese bastards if we lose this thing?"

Two remarkable events occurred on my first "recon" patrol. I was one of three rookies in a seven member recon unit led by Max. We were stealthily moving through the brush when the sound of an AK-47 cracked out – a distinct ring one never forgets - "Krack – Krack". Max, in the lead, immediately hit the ground and looked back at his new charges. He saw that we were on the deck and trying to burrow into the ground. He later remarked how quick our collective reaction time had been and was confident of our chances of survival. That is as long as we got our butts on the ground and didn't go charging off to the sounds of guns.

Later that day our patrol broke off into two teams; us rookies with Max, and the others with our squad leader Sergeant Johnson. My group broke through the bush into a clearing of swampy low grass at exactly the same time as several North Vietnamese Regulars did. "What we have here is a Mexican stand off," muttered Max to no one in particular. After an eternity of seconds, with the enemy seemingly only several meters away (it was probably closer to 30 meters). Max began gesturing methodically, the leader on the other side acted in kind and both groups began to backup, slowly withdrawing into the bush with no shots fired. Roger's Rangers had their Standing Orders, but Max had his own "Rules of Survival". Number one - "Fight if you must, but look for a way out first." We certainly learned more of his rules as the year unfolded. It was comforting to know the NVA had a Maxwell or two on their side as well.

Staff Sergeant Johnson, my squad leader decided I, standing at five foot nine inches, one hundred seventy pounds, fit the stature needed to carry the squad radio. Tall guys tended to get caught up in the low hanging vines and thick bush; and the extra twenty five pounds of the radio quickly fatigued lighter guys. I was now joined at the hip to Sergeant Johnson. As his RTO (Radio Telephone Operator), I could never be more than an arm's length away from him. While on patrol, the need for constant communication with the rest of the platoon and company was essential. This was a good opportunity to learn a new trade from a seasoned pro like Johnson.

Sergeant Johnson arrived in Vietnam with the main contingent of the 1st Brigade around September of 1965. He was a 10 year career soldier in his late 20's. He had been stationed in Germany prior to his assignment to The 1st Cav. He married a girl he met while stationed there and spoke of her often. Unlike Max, he was planning to go home after his tour was up in four months. Like Max, he instilled a sense of confidence in me. If I paid attention to their actions and commands I would come out of this O.K.

Staff Sergeant Eric Johnson came to the Army by way of Indiana. Six foot tall and about 180 pounds, he had the physique of a decathlete, those jocks who have a rare combination of speed, strength and stamina to compete in the grueling ten part Olympic event.

Like Max, he was a trusted leader and seemed to thrive on the spartan conditions of life in the boonies. Unlike Max, who reveled in telling stories and got his point across with loud and profanity laced commands, Johnson's mid western reserve would only allow for a quieter, but no less imperative directive.

Max, Johnson and the other platoon, squad and team leaders regardless of rank, were in charge but the interaction between the leaders and the troops became markedly different from the relationship with the training D.I.s. The D.I.s knew our name from the name tags on our uniform. The Black Hats at Jump School knew us by the number tape on the helmet (mine was 367). Us trainees were called recruits, or for short "cruit", jackass or worse when we screwed up. Everything is at arms length, after all they had to jam as much knowledge into our skulls as possible in a very structured but short time. The interaction in combat is symbiotic and personal, we work together in teams with a leader.

Johnson was particularly adept at navigating at night and setting up ambushes. I recall one cold, rainy and windy night occupying, with the squad and Johnson, a treeless hilltop. The Hawk, as the screaming wind was fondly known, bore into our makeshift poncho tents. Even the remarkable poncho liners that we used as blankets could not keep us warm. I was dreading my turn on guard duty, and bitching about our plight. "Why in the hell are we on this useless mountain anyway?" Sgt. Johnson, my tent mate, allowed me to rant and rave and carry on for a while. Finally he had had enough of my insatiable whining and stopped me mid belly ache. He calmly explained, "Look, you dumb ass, we are on this hill as bait. Every square inch of this hill is zeroed in with artillery. Someone at battalion is just hoping 'Charlie' hits us." I got no sleep and gained a whole new perspective that night.

Another thought raced through my mind that night and would frequently occur through the next couple of months. Warriors throughout time knew the battle was imminent at day break. They could see the enemy camp fires or see their fortifications. In ancient battles death and casualties were high. At the Battle of Cannae Hannibal's Carthaginians killed over 70,000 out of 85,000 Roman Legionnaires. What did paratroopers of the 101st and 82nd Airborne think of when they jumped into Normandy before dawn on the sixth of June, 1944, or how did the assault troops attacking the beaches at day break contemplate their fate? Napoleon called it "two o'clock courage", the ability to face your fears in the darkest and most disheartening time of night.

In the case of Vietnam, we rarely knew when a fire fight would break out. Battles were generally fought in small units – Company, Platoon, and Squad size brawls. The encounters were intense but generally brief, with little time to ponder, only to react.

Our nighttime jitters took a different form. If you gazed too much on the horizon you would swear the trees and bushes in front of your position on the perimeter were moving about like evil spirits, or worse it could be "Charlie" in camouflage closing in on us, about to attack in human waves with mortar shells blasting and bugles blaring to rattle our nerves even more. Then dawn would break and the shrubbery, to the relief of all, would return to its normal stationary roots.

Believe it or not, even war zones fall into a routine. As a friend expressed it later, "A couple of dozen moments of sheer terror, the rest of the time tension, anxiety, tedium and boredom." Our routine meant some weeks in the boonies, and a much shorter time at the Base Camp in An Khe. Camp Radcliff was home to the 1st Cav plus other support units. Each time we returned from the Bush, new and more permanent structures were replacing the tent city we had first encountered. Whatever thoughts I might have entertained about a war of short duration diminished in view of our new wooden barracks and mess hall with concrete floors.

Other things began to change with our Company in addition to the ongoing construction. Up until now, our unit had been pretty much all volunteers known as "Regular Army". Now, the first wave of non airborne draftees began to fill our ranks. This was cause for some tension. These new draftees, the Legs, non airborne and not a compliment became the subject of unnecessary harassment. The tormenting was short lived, however. Spec 4th Washington, at 6 foot 4 and 235 pounds of muscle, let it be known that anyone in the Company who was giving any of the new replacements a hard time would have to answer to him.

With the possible wrath of Washington hanging over us, the harassment evolved into good natured ribbing about lack of airborne status. Things settled down and we quickly adapted to the new reality. If anyone had a right to be upset, it was the new replacements . We all had the exact same jobs but they were paid less. All the airborne troops received a monthly jump pay bonus, despite the fact that we would probably never parachute in Vietnam.

◈   ◈   ◈

All armies, ancient and modern, must face another enemy besides the opposing combatants - the enemy being disease; typhus, dysentery, plague. Even the Great Attila had to abandon the gates of Rome because his army was decimated by an unknown sickness. In Southeast Asia, Malaria was the unseen enemy of choice.

In spite of taking my obnoxiously large weekly anti-malaria pill, I fell sick with the micro enemy. One day I fainted flat on my face into a rice paddy (I really began to hate those things) while on a routine patrol. With my Squad's help, I was revived and straggled back to camp. The Company medic took my temperature, I believe it was 106. The next couple of days were lost in a haze, but I ended up in Camp Zama Army Hospital somewhere in Japan.

I spent the next 30 days being treated and recuperating. Life was tough. Three hot meals a day, movies, and eventually passes to the neighboring town. There was also an enlisted man's club on base with slot machines, music and cold beer. A Grunts paradise. I made several friends on the hospital ward including a fast talking New Yorker, Tony Rocca. He introduced me to marijuana. Where he got it from, I don't know and didn't ask. Since I did not smoke, trying to ingest the vapor into my lungs was not as easy as Tony made it look. After coughing and gagging on the first few attempts, I finally got the hang of it. It made me feel mellow and a little silly. I began repeating myself and what everyone else was saying always followed with the declarative, "Oh! Wow!" After several marijuana episodes with Rocca and other denizens of the hospital I decided that smoking pot was a pleasant enough experience but the idea of getting high for the sake of being high and laughing at nothing in particular was not the form of relaxation I wanted to seek. A cold beer or maybe Japanese sake would make a better choice.

We were released together and sent back to Vietnam through the vast military complex at Cam Ranh Bay. The bay had a deep water port. The U. S. Navy, Air Force and Army all had bases here for supplies with air fields for all types of craft from fighter jets to cargo planes. We were both from the First Cavalry. We surprised an enlisted man whose job it was to assign us to a plane when we told him we wanted to go to Saigon, although our travel orders said An Khe. But what did he care if we went AWOL (absent without leave). He didn't, and off to Saigon Rocca and I went.

We didn't have much money, but we did have Post Exchange (PX) Ration Cards which allowed us to purchase items deemed valuable and not available to the locals such as: cameras, watches, and transistor radios. All one needed was a cooperative cab driver, which was not a problem. We sold the items for two to three times what we paid. Those transactions financed our stay in Saigon.

I have been to the major cities on the East Coast: Boston, New York, Philadelphia and Washington but it seemed odd that the next major city for me to visit would be a half world away in distance and culture. It all seemed very exotic: the clothes, food, sights and smells. My only experience in Vietnam has been the boondocks, jungle and the rural villages, where the main, or perhaps the only industry was planting and harvesting rice. The people as I perceived were subsistence farmers. The dominant apparel for men and women was black pajamas, self fashioned rubber soled sandals made from used tires, and a conical hat called a non la used to protect the farmers from the sun. The brim of the hat was wide and extended beyond the narrow shoulders of the typical Vietnamese. The only burley rednecks here were us. Since the clothing worn by the farmers was also the uniform of the Viet Cong, the difficulty of distinguishing friend from foe is evident. In the small, most remote villages the houses were a thatched roof, one room hut with a packed dirt floor. In some of the larger hamlets there were some more permanent looking structures made out of a concrete or plaster like material. Most houses had a small shrine with pictures of deceased relatives surrounded by burning incense sticks. The most prevalent aroma was the pungent smell of nuoc mam, a fish sauce, I never got used to. Whereas the rural people traveled largely on foot carrying their wares by balancing two open baskets at each end of a pole positioned on their shoulders, in Saigon the most notable mode of transportation was the motor scooter, motorbike, or bicycle. Like most cities, it was crowded with the hustle and bustle of commercial activity. The pungent aroma of nuoc mam intermingled with the exhaust fumes of the taxis and motor scooters. The vendors at the open food markets sold fruit and vegetables I knew; mangoes, papayas, plums, cabbage, carrots, cauliflower, eggplant, and a lot of unfamiliar produce; guava, lychee, potaya, bok choy, daikon, and jicamo. Fish, as in the rural areas, remained the preferred main dish. Admittedly, I am not a very adventurous diner. I like my fish from a can, as in tuna, and meat and other seafood wrapped in cellophane with the heads cut off. Luckily there were plenty of restaurants that catered to occidental taste. My favorite was a little French restaurant that served the best pizza I had tasted; with apologies to New York's Ray's, Original Ray's, or Famous Ray's Pizza Shops. Up until that time my preferred choice for pizza was Chitch's in Bound Brook, N.J. Maybe it was the Malaria or months of Army food and c-rations had influenced my taste buds. I wondered if the North Vietnamese and Viet Cong appreciate good pizza?

Across the street from this cozy bistro was the Caravalle Hotel. One of those romantic, legendary places where, I imagined, soldiers of fortune, secret agents, war correspondents, and literary types rubbed shoulders, exchanged information, and told tall tales. One would expect to see Ernest Hemingway holding court at the bar. Rocca and I would leave the interior of the hotel to our imaginations. It teemed with top brass and other officers, we deemed it unwise to enter since we were absent without leave. Any questions about what a couple of grunts were doing in a swanky place like the Caravalle Hotel could prove embarrassing.

The streets of Saigon were an oddly harmonious mix of military uniforms of all stripes; G.I.s, Aussies, some South Koreans and of course the AVRN Troops. It looked to Tony and me that there were more rear echelon troops than troops in the field. I am not sure what all of them were doing, but I thought we could use a few more of them to fill in the ranks. It might be my paranoid state of mind, but there were a lot of officers around. Maybe this is where they came upon completing their six months combat tour. With the population of Saigon at four million plus, civilians still dominated the city scape. Compared to the tall, broad and sometimes overweight westerners, the Vietnamese appeared diminutive. I am sure there were some Vietnamese who were fat, but I did not see any examples. The Vietnamese, in general, are handsome and attractive with broad, open, pleasant faces and with exotic Asian eyes. It also appeared that the rural villagers aged faster than their more cosmopolitan counterparts. The strenuous life cultivating the rice paddies and fewer medical services took its toll. The men in Saigon, for the most part, dressed like westerners with cotton, collared shirts with a square tail worn outside of trousers, shoes and manufactured sandals. Admittedly, I paid more attention to the women who mostly wore traditional garments called Ao Dai, cotton or silk calf length tunics slit up the flanks over matching pants. They came in many bright colors. The conical hat somehow seemed more decorative than those in the countryside, although I am sure they are the same.

After four days we were running low on cash, so off to the PX with our trusted cab driver and guide in tow. Leaving the PX, and just after our exchange with the driver, MPs, both ours and South Vietnamese, approached us. The South Vietnamese arrested our driver but Rocca somehow talked our way out from our MPs.

I was scared. Somehow, serving time in the Brig in South Vietnam had no appeal. I decided this adventure was over. Rocca decided to stay a little longer. I got on the first C-130 heading for the safety of An Khe and the jungle. When I reached the base the company 1st Sergeant Holland asked, "Where have you been Kelly? You are four days AWOL." I told him the truth. Roger's Rangers Standing Order number four flashed through my brain. His only reply was, "Get your gear. We're going to the boonies." Things are handled less formally in combat zones.

He was eying Hektor's splendid body, to see where it might
give way, but the rest of the skin held in the armor, broken
and splendid... yet showed where the collar-bones hold the
neck from the shoulders, the throat, where death of the soul
comes swiftly; in this place brilliant Achilles drove the spear
as he came in fury, and clean through the soft part of the
neck the spear was driven.

Homer, *THE ILIAD*

◈ ◈ ◈

S taff Sergeant Johnson rotated back to the World and my group was reassigned to Staff Sergeant Morgan's platoon. Staff Sergeant Morgan came into D Company a couple of months prior to me. Like most of our Officers and NCOs, he was determined to carry out his assigned mission and, more importantly, keep us alive. Morgan was from Connecticut, married with a young son. He had been in the Army about eight years, a Lifer who had gone through Ranger and Pathfinder Training – those brave souls who jump into combat first to mark and prepare the way for the full airborne assault. Well trained for the rigors of combat, we trusted his judgment.

I began to wonder what drove these men – Maxwell, Johnson, Morgan and others like them, to be career soldiers. I do not know their circumstances when they joined the military, but clearly they had other options now. They were smart, resourceful, others followed when they led. They all achieved their rank by merit, not seniority. Whatever their reasons; patriotism, a sense of adventure, a desire to lead an extraordinary life, surely it is not the pay. I'm thankful they exist and that they were here.

Early October, 1966 Specialist Fourth Class Frank Simpson became our new squad leader. Sp 4 Simpson grew up in Baltimore, Maryland. Tall, lanky and except for his red hair he could have been Max's younger brother. Among the last of the platoon members with one month of his tour in Vietnam left, and three months until his discharge from the Army. Calm under pressure like all good leaders. I could only hope I would remain as composed as he appeared when I had only a month to go. Simpson had a limited but working knowledge of French, very useful as a number of Vietnamese villagers also spoke French. Simpson relieved me of my RTO duties and assigned me the M-79 grenade launcher. The M-79 resembles a sawed off shot gun – about 30" in length, the single barrel was large enough to fire a 40 mm cartridge. Like a hand held mortar with a range up to 400 meters. For up close and personal encounters the M-79 had shotgun cartridges. Its main drawbacks were a slow rate of fire and the grenade was not armed until it traveled thirty meters. I liked that the M-79 gave me the ability to lob shells over the jungle canopy, no need for a clear view of where Charlie may be hiding since the shell had a casualty radius like a hand grenade. A direct hit, as with a rifle, was not necessary. The more proficient I became, the more rounds I could fire before the first one hit the ground. I also took my turn at walking point. When I pulled that assignment I carried a standard M-16 rifle.

One day the company was moving to a new position near the coast of the South China Sea. We walked through a small village and in what resembled a town square there was a large chalkboard like you would see in a high school classroom. Written on the board was anti American propaganda in English, Vietnamese and French. The legacy of French influence had not been forgotten. Later that day as we made camp not too far from that village, the company commander Captain Fletcher, decided to send in a raiding party to see if we could capture some Viet Cong. Our platoon was picked. Our leader, Lieutenant Armstrong chose Sergeant Morgan to lead our squad on the raid. It was my turn to walk point. I didn't mind taking point. During training we were taught how to set up an ambush – allow the point man to pass, cut him off, and attack the main body. I guessed the NVA and the Viet Cong had similar training. At 9:00 pm, our eyes now fully adjusted to the darkness, the squad moved towards the village. Only the stars dotted the horizon, no moon to light our way, just the compass to guide us. The lack of moon glow gave me both an eerie feeling and a sense of confidence that we would approach the hamlet undetected since Charlie could not see any better in the dark than we could.

Obviously the points job was to sniff out trouble. In this I was selfish. If we did get ambushed, I would have time to react and survive. However, I failed in my job. About half way through the village, I saw a silhouette cross my path, maybe about 10 yards ahead. I thought it was possibly a child. I stopped the column on the path. These villages didn't have roads. I reported what I saw back to Sarge. He motioned me to go farther up the path. He moved forward to check out what I saw. I slowly and carefully walked about thirty meters from the halted patrol. Moments later shots rang out and a fire fight ensued.

The gap I created from the patrol indicated clearly that I was cut off. By this time the patrol was down in a ditch lining the side of the path. I found a ditch parallel to the path I was on and began firing in the direction of the flashes from the enemies rifles. My M-16 jammed (they were famous for that). I had to continuously dislodge the spent shells from the barrel with my cleaning rod. I decided I didn't like being isolated and circled back to the remainder of the squad. All pretense of stealth was gone. I crashed through brush, tree line and wooden fencing, shouting all the time so my buddies would not shoot at me coming up behind them.

The village was about a mile from the South China Sea and we were supported by a Navy Cruiser. Simpson, the next in rank , called in fire from the ship. Most shells hit in rice paddies behind the village. It is astounding the fire power a lowly infantry squad can bring to bear at a moments notice. A Navy ship with 350 men commanded by a captain, is at the beck and call of a handful of infantry privates.

I soon learned that the shadow of a child was actually V.C. duck walking trying to avoid detection. He shot Morgan through the neck. I later learned members of our patrol killed the V.C. and dragged Sgt. Morgan into the ditch with them and tried to keep him alive but it was too late.

Lieutenant Armstrong had positioned the remainder of the platoon four hundred meters on the north side of the village as we circled around and entered from the south. They quickly moved to our aid, but the action was over in fifteen minutes. We had no other casualties. We found two V.C. with rifles and one old woman who came out of a hut with a light during the brief fight. Why she did that, I'll never know. Terrible and unjust things happen during battles when civilians are around. One of Max's rules for survival was violated - stay out of the villages. Armed soldiers, and potentially hostile civilians don't mix.

We stayed in the village that night. I slept little. I wondered what the Commanding Officer would write to Sgt. Morgan's wife and young son living at Fort Bragg in North Carolina.

Others from D Company had been killed, but Morgan's death was the first from the Platoon since my arrival. The deaths of the others were greeted with little comment. Only the thought that I'm sorry they got it but I'm glad it wasn't me. Morgan's death was personal. I only hoped we wouldn't engage in that type of operation again. I sensed a terrible resolve had come over the Platoon – at the first sign of anything unexplainable we would fire first.

I found myself contemplating my own demise. I did not fear
death as much as I wondered how it would happen. Whether here and
now in this strange place or sometime in the distant future. Would
I face it with boldness and a smile or faint hearted and a whimper. I
could only hope that when the angel of death strikes, he does with swift
surprise and I prayed my reaction would be the former. I would hate to
spend eternity knowing it was the latter.

The death of Morgan caused a reshuffling of the Company's Platoon Sergeants. The Platoon was placed in the care of Max and I was
once again under his tutelage – with a renewed interest in his rules of
survival.

It seemed we spent most of our time hiking over vine entangled
hills, wading through leech and snake infested streams, and fighting our
way through elephant grass taller than full grown men with blades that
inflicted paper like cuts on exposed flesh. Not exactly the exotic vacation imagined on that PanAm flight several months ago.

The 1st Cavalry obviously no longer uses horses to charge into
battle. The Division has been designated as air mobile. Our new beasts
of burden are helicopters, primarily the Huey. Other units in Vietnam
had them, but the Cav had the most. The Huey could carry seven combat troops, had a pilot, copilot and door gunner armed with a mounted M-60 machine gun. There was also a Huey gun ship armed with
rockets, a machine gun and a grenade launcher. The ability to fly from
one place to another did not, however, alleviate our constant ground
pounding, it merely gave our battalion and brigade commanders the
opportunity to move us quickly from one area to another for an assault
or just to hike somewhere else. The choppers also afforded us some
luxuries that our Dads and Uncles did not enjoy in the Korean War or
World War II. We had hot meals and sometimes ice cream flown to
us even in the most isolated places. It was a huge morale booster. The
biggest comfort of all, however, was knowing that if we got into trouble,
were wounded, or just plain sick there was an excellent chance of being
extracted back to the safety of An Khe.

The field medics performed admirably on wounded or infirm
troops. The thought that a fully equipped hospital was a short chopper

ride away was a welcome relief. Clearly the ability to quickly move seriously wounded men from the battle field greatly enhanced the chance of survival over that of previous conflicts. The Hueys were favorite targets of the enemy, who did not care if they were marked with the Red Cross emblem. I do not think I could praise enough the courage of the chopper crews who performed their duties tirelessly under such duress. Their casualty rates had to be high. To remove troops, wounded or otherwise, the Hueys were vulnerable to enemy fire. To load troops, usually in tight spots, they had to hover and be exposed for what must have seemed like an eternity until they were able to take off.

To refresh troops while in the field, the Company would pull Palace Guard Duty. That would generally be at Battalion Headquarters at an Artillery Fire Base. We would dig fox holes, if they weren't already there from the previous Company, around the perimeter. On one such occasion, the Company had been trekking in the hot and humid sun all day and arrived at the Fire Base dog tired in the early evening. We began to take our positions. Two men to a fox hole for guard duty, we were spread thin. The deal was to stand guard for two hours while your buddy slept and then to switch. Fatigue set in after my second round, even the rustling of trees and bushes was not enough to keep me on guard. I was shaken awake by a very angry 2nd Lt., who was the Officer of the Day. I knew I was in trouble, sleeping on Guard Duty is a serious transgression. Dawn broke as I awaited my fate. Max appeared at my position and informed me that I had been given a Company Pardon from the C. O. It turned out that over half of the guards dozed off that night. To Court Marshall us was not practical. The next night we had three men to a fox hole.

The day after the Sleeping Beauty incident, the Squad, led by Simpson, went on a routine patrol. The mission entailed scouting a valley below our artillery position and to recon a neighboring hill. The target hill, although about four hundred meters high, two thirds the height of our base camp, appeared to be more vertical than the relatively gently sloping perch the battalion now occupied. It proved to be an arduous climb as dense vegetation and thick woods impeded our progress. After an exhausting two hour hike, pulling ourselves along by grabbing onto tree vines and rocks, someone unleashed the furies of hell near the crest of the hill. The blasts proved too powerful for mere mortar shells, it was artillery. Since we didn't think the NVA had any in this area, it had to be friendly fire. Zeus was throwing thunder bolts at his own people! To the sounds of the crashing shells and our cursing, we scrambled down the hill, the shells chasing us like a pack of hungry wolves all the way.

Simpson screamed into his radio to Base Camp to end the fire mission. Finally, all fell still by the time we plummeted to the bottom. Simpson got through and no one was hit, just bumped and bruised from our tumble off the mountain. The sliding and stumbling descent, dodging boulders and trees along the way, took all of ten minutes. Its amazing how quickly one can move with the proper motivation.

Simpson went to the NCO in charge of the artillery unit and said, "Thank God you got our message and stopped the shooting." The NCO replied, "What message? We never got a message that you guys were there. Our mission was to fire twenty rounds on that hill and when the twenty rounds were up, we stopped." We were glad the mission didn't call for twenty five. My fox hole mate from the previous night, Andy Browne, muttered to me, "You don't think these Artillery guys are still pissed because we fell asleep, do you?"

We were a reconnaissance outfit – our job was to find the enemy, not fight him, call in support artillery and the regular rifle companies to deal with him. In other words, we were the smart asses in the back of the class instigating and egging on the others to get into trouble.

Our mode of operation was different than the traditional infantry company. Occasionally we would pick up random civilians for a short period of time. Often they gave us information about enemy and civilian movements and activities, and we provided a relative amount of safety for their travels. For four days three Buddhist Monks traveled with us. A Vietnamese interpreter, Sergeant Nguyen, had been assigned to us several months earlier from the South Vietnamese Army. Sergeant Nguyen stood 5'5" and weighed about 120 pounds, average for a Vietnamese male. He wore a standard ARVN uniform similar to our jungle fatigues. The same lightweight boots with rubber soles and green mesh tops, the same helmet and M-16 rifle. He looked like just another short, skinny G. I. He seemed to enjoy our hot chow and even c-rations which he spiced up with hot peppers and other seasonings. He spoke English well although with a heavy accent, then again so did us Jerseyites. We had heard stories about Buddhist Monks setting them selves on fire in a demonstration of protest against the South Vietnamese Government. We hoped they would find no cause to demonstrate their expertise in self immolation while they were with us. Sargent Nguyen assured us that the Monks had no such intentions.

Ed Kane had a notion that the Monks could read the field of energy that surrounds an individual. With Sergeant Nguyen interpreting, the Monks began to read our auras. This was probably more of an attempt to humor their hosts, than a serious exercise, but they had our attention. They began with Max, proclaiming him a ferocious and fearsome warrior who had been wounded many times, but that he would not die in battle. This last pronouncement seemed to disappoint him. I was told that I would be wounded, but not seriously, and like Max would not die in battle, At that I was not disappointed. They left out the fearsome warrior part, but maybe my aura was having a bad day. While I tend not to believe this kind of stuff, I walked gingerly and slept lightly the next few weeks just to be on the safe side of the Monk's vision.

Sergeant Nguyen worked mainly with the company headquarters staff. I had limited interaction with him. On one occasion Nguyen joined my squad on a daylight patrol into a small hamlet. His job was to interrogate the locals for information. As was often the case, the only people in the village were children and women. Nguyen cornered three girls in their late teens and began questioning them in Vietnamese, of course. As the interrogation continued he became loud and his tone agitated. Suddenly he began pointing at us. The girls started to cry, folding their hands as in prayer, and began bowing and what appeared to be pleading. Abruptly the interview stopped and the girls fled.

Nguyen came over to us smiling. He obtained the information, the whereabouts of the village men, he was seeking. He had threatened to turn the girls over to us and in all likely hood be raped or killed unless they told him what he wanted to know. I was pissed. I did not like being used, but before I could say anything Andy Browne let him know if he ever pulled a stunt like that again he would deeply regret it. Sergeant Nguyen's smile quickly faded and we solemnly walked back to camp. Later I told Max what had transpired. He responded, "Some day one of us is going to get in a world of crap monkeying around in these damn villages!" Of course he is right, but we are soldiers and go where we are told.

The encounter with the monks sparked some discussion about religion and the after life. "There are no atheists in fox holes", or so the saying from World War II goes. Whenever the brigade Chaplain showed up in the field, I was among the first in a pew, actually on a log, a rock or standing. It didn't matter if he was a Catholic Priest, Protestant Minister, or Jewish Rabbi. I was not taking any chances.

Max had, as usual, an unusual point of view. "What are you Catholics, Protestants and Jews gonna do when you die and find out the object of worship is a Great Golden Toad? I at least can say 'Well Toad, I wasn't for you, but I wasn't against you either' and the Toad will give me a pass. And then I'll put in a good word for you guys." Not the most traditional Calvinist view, but Sarge was content with it. This was Sarge's side bet on Pascal's Wager, a 17th century French mathematician, physicist, and Catholic philosopher with the point of view that the existence of God can neither be proved, or disproved through rationalization. But there is everything to gain and nothing to lose by living as if God did exist.

Some time later I caught Max in a more reflective mood, "That was a good story about the Great Golden Toad, but what do you really think?" After a short pause, he replied, "Remember your first jump and how you didn't believe you were actually going to step out of an airplane in flight. It was all some kind of joke. And how your heart pounded in your chest when the Jump Master signaled the commands and opened the door. The din of nervous troopers yelling and the Hawk screaming. Then you stepped outside and suddenly all was quiet and serene. The chute opens and you are gently floating to earth. Well, thats how I see death. A transition from the chaos to a peaceful descent." Then he grinned, "Of course, I'm a little apprehensive where I'll land."

"Don't cha know, Kelly, life would be simpler if I were an atheist, I'm sure I would still possess a moral code. After all, the Ten Commandments apply to believers and nonbelievers alike. I think it would be much too easy to shrug off my 'occasional' transgressions if in the end I only had to answer to myself. No, it is much better to love God and be on edge waiting His judgment than not."

A hero is no braver than the ordinary man,
he is just brave five minutes longer.

Ralph Waldo Emerson

Sometimes I had the full measure;
sometimes I came up a couple of minutes short.

Unknown Paratrooper

I had led several small patrols in the daylight before, but this was my first night excursion as leader. Nervous doesn't begin to describe my mood. Max briefed me on where and when to go. As with most patrols the "why" eluded me. We were assigned a Forward Observer. The F.O.s job is to call in artillery or mortar fire on prearranged map coordinates. Our company was the Perimeter Guard for an artillery unit camped outside a village. My patrol mission was to set up an ambush at a predetermined spot in the village. Imagine how the local village dwellers must have felt with a bunch of over sized foreigners, with enough fire power to flatten the village in minutes, roaming between huts. Even if they were friendly to the South Vietnamese Government, we were never sure who was or was not, it had to be slightly unnerving.

Within an hour I realized, as did everyone else, we were hopelessly lost. The F. O., a supposed expert, was even more of a novice than I. After stumbling around for several hours we missed our deadline to be in position. We made a call to Head Quarters to get us back on track. The artillery unit fired a smoke shell at a designated map coordinate. When I saw the flash of the exploding round as it hit the ground I took a compass reading, next I took another compass reading at a prominent hill behind the village that I could pin point on the map. The intersection of the two compass readings told me we were still one thousand meters from our destination, a long and forbidding hike in the dark. At this point if there were any V.C. out there we were more likely to be the ambushee than the ambusher.

The C.O. ordered us to go on. I refused. My squad was happy with that decision. I would face the consequences in the morning. I gambled it would be hard to explain at the Court Martial Hearing why a lowly Private First Class was leading a dangerous night patrol from a Company that had several Officers and Sergeants available. Max chewed me out when we made it back. He used language only a grizzled veteran could muster – grinning the whole time. The C.O. issued an order that Privates could no longer lead patrols. Two weeks later I was promoted to Specialist 4th Class – a rank equivalent to a Corporal.

After about eight months I became a full fledged squad leader along with Palmer who came into the platoon with me. We were still Spec 4's but all of the platoon's original members, except Max of course, had rotated home.

One thing different about this war, you knew how long you would be in Vietnam - one year - as opposed to WWII when you served for the duration. Officers, on the other hand, served for six months in the field. I do not know where they went after that, perhaps they went home, or to a desk job somewhere. As a result, we served with two or three Lieutenants as Platoon Leaders and two or three Company Commanders. They led us well as our casualties were fairly low and they had the respect of the NCOs in the company. Only two instances involving two of our platoon leaders stand out in my memory.

Our company was involved in a Battalion size operation late in the afternoon and through the night. There was a lot of shooting yet no casualties I could note in our corner of the fight. When night fell it was quite spectacular. The red bullet tracers from our M-16s criss-crossing with the green tracers from the NVA's AK-47s. My squad was tucked safely behind rice paddy dikes separating the fields. When morning broke all seemed quiet. Then the Platoon Leader ordered us to line up, about three yards between men. We stood up in an open field, our next move to assault the village where the NVA had been firing from. The 100 meters to the village felt like 1,000. The field was open with our only salvation another rice paddy dike about half way to the village.

In the age of jet fighters, guided missiles, helicopters and artillery that could fire with pinpoint accuracy from thirty miles, we were about to duplicate Pickett's Charge at Gettysburg. Despite our apprehension of pending doom, the Lieutenant stood up and shouted, "fix bayonets!", and led us forward. We dutifully followed. Sometimes in a desperate fight where there is no retreat the only thing left to do is stand up and attack regardless of the outcome. This, however, did not feel like that kind of situation. As we crossed the point of no return the Lieutenant couldn't take the tension any more and yelled, "Charge!" We all ran to the village. If we were going to die it would be at double time and not cowering in the dry bedded rice paddy.

Dripping in sweat and fear, we reached the village. Our greeting was not with a hale of bullets from Charlie, but one old papasan sitting in a chair in front of his hut. Smiling and waving, welcoming us like visiting friends and relatives.

Apparently the NVA decided to leave, thinking we would call in artillery. Even they couldn't believe we would be dumb enough to do what we did. Thank God somebody had some sense.

After my night patrol screw up I was determined not to get lost again. I studied our maps diligently. We all knew we were in the Central Highland Region, but exactly where at any given time was a mystery. Our world consisted of about 10,000 meters (10K) on a map. How that related to the larger picture was not our concern. We spent our time looking for signs of the V.C. from one point on the map to another.

On one such excursion our Squad was being led by a newly commissioned Lieutenant fresh from Officer Candidate School (OCS). Lt Miller was a mustang. A mustang is a wild horse, not a thoroughbred. In the Army it meant one who became an officer by moving up through the enlisted ranks, not by the preferred method of attending West Point or a college ROTC program. A mustang might be missing the polish achieved at the academies or college but in general I think their experience as enlisted men gives them a more practical knowledge and instinct at our level. His map and compass skills, however, were in need of help. Several times I tried to point out that we were off course but he just brushed me aside. Overcoming his ego, he realized he was lost, and quietly asked me if I knew our location. I quickly showed him and pointed us in the right direction. I knew just how he felt.

He obviously did some serious map studying after that outing. He never got lost again while I was in his Platoon. That was only a couple of months. I was short. In the Army that is a term for time not stature. My tour would soon be over.

The Ides of March fell upon us and I along with Palmer and Anderson began our countdown, sixty days until I rotated home. Andy Browne, a squad leader like us, cheated. He contracted malaria. Since it took thirty days to recover from the disorder we knew Browne would likely not be back.

Andy managed a smile and a weak wave of farewell through the alternating chills and fever as he was med evac'd from the field. We managed to stifle our jealousy and get on with the tasks ahead. Max now needed to appoint, or more correctly recommend, a new squad leader to Lieutenant Carter. His pick, like ours, was Spc 4 Ron Tharp, a street smart leg draftee from Philadelphia and a fire team leader since February. He always had a good story and was quick to laugh at the stories of others. He was well liked by all. More importantly, he was calm under pressure, had good map skills, and when things got tough you wanted him in your fox hole.

When Max approached him about the job, Tharp inexplicably turned it down. Maybe he did not want the added responsibility or maybe just a temporary loss of self confidence. Whatever the cause Max, not accustomed to being rejected, persisted,"Listen Dumb ass, I can't make you take the job but if you don't I'll give it to Davis and you can take orders from him!" Bill Davis, not a bad guy, but not up to the task of leadership. Under the threat of being led by Davis, Tharp relented.

It then occurred to me, half way around the world, Anderson, Palmer, Tharp and I were now the old guard. Twenty one and twenty two year old grizzled veterans. Later that night I told Max he used a risky bluff. Max replied, "I only bluff in front of officers."

And so, dear boy, I made my way home from Troy,
in total ignorance, knowing nothing of their fates,
the ones who stayed behind: who escaped with
their lives and who went down.

King Nestor, *THE ODYSSEY*

The first week of May, 1967 I was issued two sets of orders. The first was a promotion to Sergeant E-5. The second, and more important, traveling orders back to "The World" - the USA! I was assigned to the 82nd Airborne at Fort Bragg, N. C. and had a 30 day leave before I had to report. I am sure there was some sort of out processing in An Khe. All I remember is getting on a military transport with the other 15 or so guys I came to the 1st Cav with. Our class "A" uniforms were not in the best shape after sitting in our overseas bags for one year but we didn't care. We were heading home. I believe everyone was smiling the entire trip from An Khe to Ton Son Nhat Air Base in Saigon.

Our airborne taxi, Braniff International, evidently had a different view of travel. Our plane was bright orange on the exterior with a large B I logo on its white tail. This was a marked departure from the olive drab military and staid silver civilian aircraft on which we flew previously. What we encountered in the interior of the plane really grabbed our full attention. Combat troops who had not seen too many women over the last year were suddenly greeted by beautiful, mini skirted stewardesses who now referred to each other as "hostesses". True, we had all seen mini skirts at parties and occasionally on the city streets, but not as part of a work uniform. I wondered what other changes I would meet.

The hostesses began the usual preflight instructions which no one heard, we were too busy gawking as the ladies moved up and down the aisle; interesting how guys can not stare and hear at the same time. A few moments later a friendly greeting by the pilot. The fasten seat belts sign flicked on. We all held our breath as the plane rumbled down the runway. As it became airborne a raucous cheer went up. We were actually leaving. On to San Francisco.

We landed at an air base in Oakland. Here we were issued new dress uniforms to travel home in. Women at sewing machines stitched on our patches, rank insignias. Service ribbons and badges were issued all in accordance with our travel orders. Very efficient. Transformed from the bedraggled, unkempt, fresh from the jungle and fourteen hour flight of two hours earlier, we now looked the part of sharply dressed soldiers. Now to San Francisco International Airport.

The 150 of us that left Viet Nam together began to dwindle as Troopers caught planes to L.A., Chicago, Minneapolis, Louisville, New Orleans and so on. I was headed to Philadelphia. I could have caught a plane to Newark, but that was two hours later and I wasn't going to wait. I was restless and filled with the need to keep moving. Afraid if I stood still too long some officer would say a mistake had been made and send me back to that damnable jungle. The further from the Pacific Coast the better.

It was a normal commercial flight, not Braniff. That disappointment aside, an all together pleasant journey. There were several soldiers on the crowded plane, two of whom had gone through A.I.T. and Jump School with me but had then been assigned to different units in Viet Nam. It was fun to get reacquainted. We talked mostly about what we were going to do. The consensus of activities revolved around bars, girls, and trips to the Jersey shore for more bars and girls, and very little about what we had done. The Stewardesses fed us drinks for free and by the end of the flight we were all somewhat less than sober. We said our goodbyes and made empty promises to keep in touch. I managed to find my way on to a bus heading for New Brunswick, New Jersey.

Random thoughts roamed my semiconscious mind. "I took the road less traveled by, and that made all the difference." Robert Frost. Max's version, as usual, was much more practical than Frosts', "If you want to keep your young ass alive never walk on a beaten trail, make your own path; and never return the same way you went." I thought that was good advice even if you were not worried about an ambush.

My parade of memories continued. I thought of one dark morning after hiking through the bush, up hills with 50 pounds of gear (weapons and food) on our backs. Everyone fighting their own battle against an unrelenting antagonist, mosquitoes. The eerie stillness of the night would be interrupted with a loud slapping sound as one trooper after another, unable to endure his tormentor would strike a blow on his own face or neck. During the day it was pesky flies or ants that continued mini assaults on our flesh. The insect world also had a navy, leeches! Any time we would wade through a river, a stream, or many times walking through a knee high flooded rice paddy, leeches would find the most unique and vulnerable places to latch on to. Pulling the leeches off was useless as their heads would just break apart from their bodies since they had such a powerful grip on your skin. The only way to remove a leech is to light a match to its tail or pour mosquito repellent on it so it recoils and loses its grip. At 3:00 a.m. our Company reached it's destination. I began assigning guard duty when one of my squad members, Whitey, noticed I had not assigned myself a time. Somewhere in my mind I had decided it was my privilege as exalted honcho to rest while others pulled duty. Whitey was a Spc 4 and the last of the early members of our Company with only a month to go. He was an excellent field soldier. The kind that belongs in the boonies. Back at An Khe he was always running into trouble. A very strong, independent streak, if you will. He had enough of my bloated sense of entitlement and laid his verbal beating on me as quietly as possible. Yelling at night in the middle of hostile country is not wise. My ego deflated, knowing I acted like a real jerk, I meekly submitted and took my turn on duty. Humbled, but somewhat wiser.

I remembered a python we tripped over while on recon patrol one muggy day near a wide, stone filled stream. The snake was lurking in a thick, grassy area near the stream. The point man stepped on it and the serpent reacted with a loud hiss and large, opened jaws that could swallow a small dog. The reptile was at least twenty feet long. Its' head was an uneven trapezoid form with a light tan V-shape marking that extended from its blunt snout above the eyes to the beginning of its sleek and tapered body. At its widest point the midsection was half the size of a telephone pole. The snake's torso was camouflage in brown irregular blocks about two inches outlined by the same light tan color on the head. Kane, Palmer and I picked it up and began carrying the monster to the stream about ten meters away. The skin had a leathery feel, not slimy to the touch as I had expected. Immediately the python began to constrict around us, as if we were prey to be squeezed into submission. Although the beast weighed about one hundred and fifty pounds and was all muscle, it could not match our collective strength and soon began attempts to free itself from our grasp with powerful contractions. When we reached the stream we released the snake and it slithered to the safety of the water. In my early teenage years, my Mother's brothers, Sean and Phil, would take me deer hunting in the woods of New Jersey, yes New Jersey has forests and trees. I loved being with them, the camping out and tracking the deer. But when given the opportunity to shoot, I could never pull the trigger. Somehow killing animals in the wild when food was not a concern seemed senseless. Inexplicably, as the snake began moving downstream, we opened fire and killed it. Instantly remorse set in as our target sank to the bottom. I prayed that God would forgive this senseless act.

The bus rumbled into Princeton, its last stop before our final destination of New Brunswick. While waiting for the exchange of passengers I thought of an intense encounter on a three man long range reconnaissance patrol with Sergeant Johnson, Simpson and me as the RTO. We repelled out of the Huey from ropes at about twenty feet from the ground. This allowed the chopper to move out quickly, just in case it was spotted. We were to hike over a two hundred meter high hill and observe if a suspected NVA Battalion was moving through the valley on the opposite side of our position. After about an hour perched under cover we observed movement in the valley. It was, however, monsoon season and fog and rain set in. Johnson called our observation into H. Q. and we began to slowly retreat back to our drop off point to be picked up. Half way down we could not see through the fog and mist, but heard large numbers of Vietnamese chattering. Another NVA unit of undetermined size had moved into that valley and it seemed they were slowly moving up the hill. We were surrounded. Johnson guessed, as we quietly moved back to the top, that the two units were going to link and we, undetected so far, would be caught in the middle. Sarge coolly called for our chopper to pick us up at a map coordinate on the top of the hill. After twenty minutes, with me in silent prayer promising God I would become a Priest if he let us escape, we heard the wack-wack of the choppers blades cutting through the haze. Of course the NVA could hear it also. The window of our escape was closing fast. Johnson popped a colored smoke grenade, the color varied daily, this day it was yellow, so the enemy could not use the same color to trick helicopters into landing in the wrong spot. The smoke was useless, however, as it dissipated into the mist about fifteen meters up. Johnson had to talk the pilot down. When he guessed the chopper was directly overhead he told the pilot he had visual contact. He lied and I'm sure the pilot did not believe him but the gutsy pilot kept coming down anyway. At the fifteen meter mark we could see it and they could now see the ground. The NVA were firing blindly at the sound of the chopper blades. Once the pilot could see, the barren hilltop made an excellent landing zone, but it also made us very vulnerable to the enemy, who I believe were about to burst through the mist. The chopper never touched ground and the three of us used our best Olympic high jump techniques to leap for the chopper's landing struts and were pulled up into the Huey by the gunner and crew chief. We thanked the crew profusely through our smiles of relief. The pilot remarked, "I'm glad to be of service." As I listened to the comforting sounds of the blades whipping through the now clear air, I wondered if I had the courage to do what this crew did. As the full bus thundered north on U.S. Route #1, I prayed the Almighty's understanding that the priestly promise was made under extreme duress and would release me from my rashness.

The path to New Brunswick was clearly marked with familiar and pronounceable names on sign posts; Kingston ten miles, Kendall Park eighteen miles. Only an occasional red light to impede our progress. No need to orient the map and compass to stay on course, the bus driving point man knew the way.

With no one to serve me drinks, I drifted off to a pleasant nap for the next half hour. I woke up at the bus stop, it wasn't a station, just the main street in New Brunswick, where I would pick up another bus for home. It was night, maybe 8:00 P.M. The bus stop was near a local pub. Having a slight hangover there was no desire to enter. One of the locals strode out of the bar and spotted me in uniform standing with about three or four other people waiting for the bus. It was embarrassing. First he offered me drinks. When I declined, he offered me money. He tried to hand me a $100 bill. I thought about taking it. Maybe there is something to being a conquering hero. Maybe the other people at the bus stop would chip in too. Reality and the bus arrived in time to save the guy's money and my dignity. For the first time in a long time I again felt out of step with my surroundings.

My slight hangover was giving way to a sense of excitement to see my parents, brothers and sister. The trip to North Plainfield took about one hour and our house was about a block from the bus stop. North Plainfield is a small, middle class community. Most of the residents are skilled workers. My Dad was a tool and dye maker, friends' parents were small business owners, teachers, accountants, middle managers for local companies. Some Dads took the one and one half hour commute to New York City by bus or train. Our house was a two bedroom ranch with a basement and an expansion attic. It was typical of the homes that went up across the country after World War II. With the help of a few uncles, my Dad raised the roof and added two more bedrooms upstairs when my sister, Janet, was born.

At last the bus halted at my stop. As I paced off the hundred yards or so to our home, I realized it was the first time in a long time that I walked that far without someone in front of me or trailing behind me. I had not called home in advance, so my arrival was a shock to my family. There were plenty of tears and hugs, but few words to go around. My adrenalin wearing down, a deep sense of relief and fatigue set in. All I wanted to do was go to sleep in my comfortable bed. But not before my sister reminded me of my promise to visit her fourth grade class at St. Peter's Grammar School. Her classmates had written to me often during my tour.

After a day of rest and home cooking, I donned my uniform and went off to St. Peter's to thank Janet's class for their thoughtfulness. There, I was greeted by the class teacher, a Nun, Sister Theresa. The same Sister Theresa who had threatened to "box my ears" every time I escaped to the day dreams in "Matt World" when I was in her class thirteen years before. Never quite sure what a "boxed ear" looked like and not wanting to find out, Sister had my full attention, at least for a while. She seemed much smaller and friendlier than I remembered, but no less intimidating, it must be her uniform, I was still outranked. I found it was just as awkward standing in front of a classroom as it was to be a student sitting in the classroom and being called on to answer a question about which I hadn't a clue. I don't remember what I said, other than "thank you", but after I spoke my sister was beaming and her classmates clapped. As I said goodbye I had a momentary impulse to ask Sister Theresa just what exactly entailed a boxed ear, but I thought better of it and left. As I departed the school grounds I realized I had left the jungle behind over a week ago. This was the longest stretch of time that my feet and boots were not waterlogged, caked in mud or some other undefinable sludge. There would no longer be a need to carry two extra pairs of socks along with ammo and c-rations.

It was late spring of 1967 and many of my high school friends were returning from college. Most of them had graduated and there was talk of MBAs, Law School and jobs they had lined up. Some were talking about or already planning weddings.

It seemed our paths would take us in different directions, at least for a while. I had about eighteen months of active duty left to serve. Right now I had twenty eight days of leave and freedom left and I planned to party hard. Nights of beer, women and rock & roll filled my vision. There were plenty of parties to attend and bars to visit. But it seemed that after a few rounds, well maybe more than a few, my body had other ideas. All it wanted to do was sleep. Often I would just doze off where I sat. Max had said, "War on occasion will test your courage, but will constantly try your endurance." My body, after a year of tension and sleep deprivation, had endured enough and wanted to recuperate. Every now and then, however, the spirit would triumph. My leave was dwindling down to the last couple of days. I had a strange desire to get down to Fort Bragg. Not unlike when as a kid and summer was coming to an end. I hated school but looked forward to the structure of the routine, to rejoin my classmates and see what the new year would bring. I was happy to see my friends setting off on a new adult adventure of work, marriage and career, but I was content to see what new adventures the 82nd Airborne would offer.

CHAPTER III

Boring can be Good

I arrive at Fort Bragg, Fayetteville, N. C. behind the wheel of my brand new Pontiac Firebird 400 – a glorious machine. My Dad said it did 95 mph just sitting in the driveway. It had a racing stripe on the side and a tachometer mounted on the hood. Of course I had no idea what a tachometer was or why it was necessary, but I had one. I paid cash for the machine with the money I saved from my tour. With a tach on the hood it's more than a mere car, it's a machine. I guess I hadn't really matured a lot. I could have kept that money for eventually returning to college but I felt I had earned a treat.

I was assigned to the 325th with a number of other newly promoted Buck Sergeants from Vietnam. The parking lot was populated with a lot of new cars; Chargers, GTOs, Malibus, Mustangs, but no tachs on the hood. All new never the less.

Life at Bragg wasn't bad. The food at the Company Mess Hall was good. There was a fair amount of time off between duties. It was only an eight hour drive home. Myrtle Beach wasn't far. I went home with friends to Virginia Beach and Kentucky. Some buddies had friends and girl friends at the Universities in North Carolina.

However, it was still the Army. We trained constantly. The 82nd had at least one Battalion on alert at all times. This meant that when it was your Units turn you were confined to the base and one Company in that Battalion was confined to the Company Barracks Area.

We got to jump frequently. The thought of jumping gave me butterflies. Not much different from those I had before playing a football game or running in a track meet. Oddly, I never had them before a lacrosse match. The anxiety wasn't as bad as what I felt before a math test. Exhilaration and awe flowed through me to be part of a couple hundred Paratroopers descending from the clouds.

Up until now my only experience with Army life had been training or wandering aimlessly in Southeast Asia. I was about to take part in a new military ritual called Breaking Starch. In basic training our uniforms were fatigues – work clothes – olive drab in color and standard cotton in textile. I had noticed that the Drill Instructors uniforms were significantly sharper and crisper in appearance than those of us mere trainees. In Vietnam we wore jungle fatigues. They were light weight material and loose fitting. They had lots of large blousey pockets on both shirts and pants. The shirts were not tucked in to the pants and had two pockets in front to hang below the belt line. I didn't like the feeling of untuckedness. After a while I began ripping the pockets off the bottom of my shirts and neatly tucking my shirt in to my pants. If the V. C. were to kill or capture this Yankee Imperialist Running Dog, at least they might note that I was a very dapper Yankee Imperialist Running Dog.

Here at Fort Bragg we took our fatigues to the local laundries where they would be cleaned and then pressed with concrete like starch. This gave the fatigues the appearance of being made of cardboard. To get your arms and legs in, you literally had to chisel your way through the starch.

Some of the senior N.C.O.s changed their uniforms twice a day. They looked good but using up to twelve uniforms a week got a little expensive. Us Buck Sergeants usually got by on one uniform a day. To keep the wrinkles under control we tried not to move or bend our arms and legs too much. Life at Bragg quickly fell into a routine mixture of spit and polish (mainly the barracks and company grounds), physical training, full gear forced marches, time at the rifle range, sharpening our land navigation skills, and an occasional parachute jump. Not unlike nine to five, more like six to six, jobs. The tension that heightened our awareness in Vietnam had dissipated. I for one had lost my edge.

The Army had a policy that unless you volunteered you only served one Tour of Duty in Vietnam. A popular refrain used when you thought about bending the rules was, "What are they going to do, send me to Vietnam?" That was the worse they could do, and they couldn't do it. This led to a serious attitude problem by some of us Junior N.C.O.s. Some of us started to goof off. Nothing major, just not always being wherever, or doing whatever was required.

The company First Sergeant was aware that things were not going well with some of us and decided to have a little talk with all new Buck Sergeants. Top was a Korean and Vietnam Vet. A good soldier and a good man. We all had great respect for him. He was also very succinct, "In the Army we have Non Commissioned Officers and Sergeants. I know you all think they are the same. Well not quite, you see N.C.O.s take the responsibility and privilege of rank and Sergeants only want the privilege and dodge the responsibility. Now if some of you Sergeants don't shape up, you will no longer be either."

The next morning I had head count duty at the Mess Hall. The importance of counting the number of troops coming in for breakfast eluded me. The other part of that duty was to keep the chow line running smoothly and, as military protocol requires, to yell "Attention!" when an officer enters the room. Well, the Battalion Commander., Lt. Col. Smith, came in and completely caught me off guard. It was unusual for the Colonel to enter the mess hall.. I did let out a weak "attention", as one of the senior N.C.O.s let me know later while trying not to laugh. The Colonel responded "As you were men" to the few troops who had actually heard me. He then asked to see the head count tally which, of course, I wasn't keeping. His next words chilled my very soul, "Report to me at Battalion Head Quarters right after company formation."

After Top's talk the day before I had decided I liked being an N.C.O. and was going to make the effort to take the responsibility seriously. Ironically now I was getting busted because I couldn't count. God I hated math.

The Colonel chewed me out. His comments were a lot like Top's. I got the point and for some reason he didn't bust me. He just had the Battalion Sergeant Major assign me to extra weekend duties for a month. I was grateful and lucky.

An old Army saying is, "never volunteer". To the contrary, I volunteered a lot. I would try anything to escape the day to day duties of Garrison life. Training exercises and jumps were fine, but when we weren't doing those, there was a lot of busy work. Nothing like leading a bunch of elite paratroopers on a detail to pick up cigarette butts. The old Roman Legions, when they were not conquering some hapless tribe, at least built roads. So volunteering seemed a better option. Most of these boredom breaking sojourns were interesting.

One early Spring morning at Company Formation Top asked for two N.C.O.s for a two or three day mission. He never told what the mission was before hand, just how long. I quickly stepped out as did my friend Sgt. Jones, another volunteer aficionado. Top told us we were going to Fort Riley in Kansas to pick up a trooper who had gone AWOL – Absent Without Leave. He had been captured, and was being held in the Brig there. We were to escort him back, in handcuffs, to Bragg for Court Marshall. We were issued side arms, 45 cal. Pistols; handcuffs; traveling money and commercial airline boarding passes. I was hoping for Braniff but they were not the airline of record from Fayetteville, N.C. to Manhattan, Kansas.

We arrived late in the afternoon and reported to the Brig Head Quarters. The Clerk in charge told us the C. O. was gone for the day, but we could pick up our lost soul in the morning at 8:00 when he would be back. So far, so good. We had planned on an overnight stay anyway. We booked a room at a hotel in Manhattan and began searching for a place to party. After all this was a college town, home of Kansas State University. With the help of our cab driver we managed to find a couple places to go. It was nice to see a bunch of people our age who were not in uniform and were having a good time. We had a good time but didn't stay out too late since we had an early morning appointment.

We arrived back at Fort Riley and reported to the Brig. We were greeted by the Clerk from the previous day. He immediately ushered us into the C.O.s office, Captain Myers. He was visibly nervous and fidgeting. Somewhat disheveled, it looked like he had slept in his uniform. Our difference was stark. We had on our Class "A" uniforms. The green jacket and pants, and tan shirt and tie of Airborne Soldiers are the same as all Army personnel. We, however, get to accessorize. We wear overseas caps, a soft foldable headgear with straight sides that split over your skull. Troopers would flatten down the crown so peaks would be visible on the front and rear with Airborne emblem; a circular patch outlined in red, blue background with a stitched replica of a deployed parachute and glider plane, not those ugly round saucer-like hats. Our jump boots are highly polished with our pant leg tucked inside, v. s. low quarters, standard Army shoes. We never actually jump with them on, all the dust or mud when you hit the ground screws up the shine. Add on our insignias, combat and service ribbons, and the pistols strapped to our sides and you have the ultimate power suit. We stood in sharp contrast to the hapless Captain.

Our sartorial splendor was not the only reason for his discomfort. It seems our prisoner was not available. He was on a two day pass from prison. My partner reacted calmly, quickly and respectfully, "Sir, you mean you gave someone who may be Court Marshalled for desertion a pass?" We both stifled our laughter while looking as stern and menacing as possible. The chagrined officer assured us our charge would be back the next day. This was good news for us. Another night of freedom.

The following morning we returned to the base to find our prisoner waiting in the office with a Sergeant in charge. There was no sign of Captain Myers and we didn't ask for him. The Sergeant had a sly grin on his face, seemingly aware of what had transpired the previous day and relishing in the C.O.s embarrassment.

We exchanged a few words with the Sergeant, signed some papers, and handcuffed our prisoner. A jeep appeared to taxi us to the airport. My partner and I decided the prisoner was not going to escape so, at the airport, we uncuffed him and put our pistols in our over night bags. Back to Bragg. Mission accomplished.

CHAPTER IV

They Said it Couldn't be Done

I called back with another burst of anger, 'Cyclops if any man on the face of the earth should ask you who blinded you, shamed you so – say Odysseus, Raider of Cities, he gouged out your eye, Laertes' son who makes his home in Ithaca.

Odysseus, *THE ODYSSEY*

Hear me Poseidon, god of the sea blue mane who rocks the earth! If I really am your son and you claim to be my Father – come, grant that Odysseus, Raider of Cities, Laertes' son who makes his home in Ithaca, never reach home.

The Cyclops Polyphemus, *THE ODYSSEY*

In mid November the Battalion began to form Long Range Reconnaissance Patrol Teams (LRRPS – pronounced Lurps). They were generally three men teams trained and equipped to move undetected for several days to pinpoint enemy strength and movements. I had been on a few similar patrols with the Cav and thought this would be an interesting way to finish up my last year of service. Staff Sergeant Lucas Shelby, the head of my team, was a Vietnam veteran who served with the Special Forces (Green Berets), an intelligent and professional soldier in his late twenties, also a remarkable artist. I still have some excellent pen and ink sketches he gave me.

Under Shelby's tutelage Joe Evans, another Buck Sergeant from the 1st Cavalry, and I refined our land navigation skills and improved our camouflage techniques. Shelby taught us how to effectively throw a knife. One set of skills he was a little apprehensive to teach us nonprofessionals, British Commando Maiming Tactics. He knew most of us wouldn't reenlist, although he often tried to talk me into it. The name speaks for itself. It is comprised of a series of surprisingly easily learned simple moves designed to permanently disable an opponent. My favorites; how to poke out an eye, how to smash a kneecap, and why hitting an opponent with the heel of your hand is way more effective than a rolled up fist. These moves along with several others comprised the ultimate marshal art.

Shelby claimed to be worried about us getting into barroom brawls. He needn't be concerned. As in most things in life, execution is the key. After a few beers, focus and coordination become an issue. The patrons of the local pubs were safe enough.

Early February, 1968 I managed to wrangle a prized three day pass and drove the ten hours back home; the agenda, a visit with family, and then a party at Allen Richmond's apartment building. Allen was now in his first year of law school after graduating from the University of Pennsylvania where he played football and lacrosse. A good student and athlete who overcame whatever short comings in talent with sheer determination and an extraordinary work ethic. It came as no surprise to me after dinner that Allen decided to study a couple hours more before joining me at the neighbors' gathering. His annoying work first, party later attitude could be the reason he is in law school and I'm in a uniform. I arrived back at Bragg late that Sunday night.

The barracks were unusually active for that time of night. The Sergeant on night duty handed me orders assigning me to the 508th along with about half of the N.C.O.s and troops from our Company. Something big was happening. I packed my bag and drove over to the 508th area. There I met up with several buddies from different companies, including Shelby.

It was the 508th turn to be on ready alert. Like most Army units at that time, it was not up to full strength in personnel. Troops from other units were called in to fill the gap. This was clearly not a training exercise. The 508th was the Brigade sent to Detroit when riots broke out on July 23, 1967. The riots started when the police raided an unlicensed, black after hours club and tried to arrest all of the 80 plus patrons. Ironically, the gathering was celebrating the return of two local soldiers from Vietnam. After two days of mayhem, it became obvious the police and the National Guard, called in by Governor Romney, were overwhelmed by the situation. It was the third time in my memory that airborne troops were called into a local racial problem. First, President Eisenhower sent the 101st airborne to escort black children to integrate Little Rock Central High School in Arkansas in 1957. In 1962 President Kennedy sent the 503rd military police airborne battalion to stop the rioting segregationists at the University of Mississippi when James Meredith enrolled as the first black student.

The arrival of a thousand or more well armed and disciplined paratroopers, many of whom were combat vets, with no intention of being shot at in an American city, proved to be enough show of force to end the destruction. Forty eight hours after their deployment, the 508th returned to Bragg. No casualties reported.

Some of the Troopers took their next three day pass and went back to Detroit. The people in the surrounding towns viewed them as heroes. They were treated like royalty. They couldn't buy a meal or drink the whole time. Some admitted it was the first time they wore their uniform off duty.

We were on alert, and we were going somewhere, and it wasn't Detroit or anywhere else in the U. S. The speculation revolved around

Israel, Korea, and Vietnam. The Mideast was still a hot spot. Eight or nine months earlier the Israelis kicked the butts of Syria, Egypt and Jordan in the Six Day War. It didn't seem likely that those countries were ready to take on Moshe Dyan and Israel again considering the beating the Israelis handed them, I didn't think Israel needed our help. The Communists from North Korea had just captured one of our Navy vessels, The Pueblo, and had killed several of the crew members. The Pueblo was in international water at the time. The North Koreans claimed otherwise. In Vietnam, the Marine Base at KheSanh, near the DMZ, was under heavy assault. There were also reports of strong NVA and VC attacks throughout the south, including Saigon in the south and the Ancient Imperial City of Hue in the northern province of South Vietnam, later to be known as The Tet Offensive of 1968.

Things were moving fast. I estimated that about 150 troops from other units within the 82nd reported to the 2nd Battalion of the 508th. I'm sure a like number of troops filled in the ranks of the 1st and 3rd Battalions of the 508th. To integrate this many men at once into new units was highly unusual and only heightened our apprehension as to what our mission would entail. I was assigned as a Squad Leader to a Platoon with a West Pointer, a brand new 2nd Lieutenant, and Shelby as his Platoon Sgt. With Shelby as part of the team, our new Lieutenant would have excellent guidance for whatever we were going to do.

We had a couple of hours off to take care of personal effects, most importantly our new cars. Several of us left our cars at the home of a married friend, Sgt. Josh Allen, who lived off base. Allen and I had served together in the Cav. This must have been very stressful for his new wife. Her husband was being shipped out to God knows where, for who knew how long, and she was in charge of a fleet of strangers cars. My brother, Paul, came to pick up my car several days after we deployed. Later I found out that my Mom had commandeered the machine and had gotten a speeding ticket. I wonder if she knew what a tachometer was for?

The speculation of our destination ended abruptly when we saw mosquito nets among the gear issued. I suspect Israel and Korea have mosquitoes, but we knew we were scheduled for a return trip to Vietnam. The loop hole in that Army Directive about one tour in Vietnam meant an individual soldier could not be singled out, that could be construed as punishment or personal animosity. Sending an entire unit, however, was not personal. How we were chosen to be transferred to this particular battalion is another question.

The C. O. held a Company formation to give us the official word: Vietnam. About half of the newly formed Company were combat veterans and took the news in stride. Secretly, some of us were not that disappointed about going back. Garrison Duty was boring. Something adventuresome and exhilarating existed roaming about the bush and encountering the enemy. The C.O. explained that 6,000 Marines and 3,000 Paratroopers were part of a reinforcement effort to stem the NVA offensive and help relieve the pressure at Khe Sanh.

I view Marines as proud and brave and, like Paratroopers, share the temperament of the Spartans. Spartan warriors, before going into battle were admonished by their women to come home either carrying their shield or on it. Simply put, the Spartan's shields were so large and heavy that in order to flee from the fight one would have to discard it. To be carried back in death upon the shield signified the Spartans did not leave their dead on the battle field, nor would Marines or Paratroopers. The stubborn spirit of the Spartans was clearly on display at the pass of Thermopylae in 480 B.C. Secretly, I was jealous of the Marine Corp Motto "Semper Fidelis", Always Faithful. Easily understood and a catchy phrase. The Motto of the 82nd Airborne, "Airborne ...All The Way", slightly cumbersome and vague.

We left Pope Air Base, next to Fort Bragg, two days after our initial alert in an Air Force C141 Stratojet, one of the planes from which we parachuted. We didn't actually jump as we did from a C130 Hercules, a four engine prop. From the C141 it was more like a step out and then the Hawk would snatch you. A very different sensation. But alas, again no Braniff.

My earlier bravado about returning to combat began to fade as we came closer to our destination. I thought of Odysseus from the legend of the Trojan War. Odysseus, the Raider of Cities, whose cunning and courage led to the destruction of ancient Troy.

Odysseus, blown off course on his return voyage from conquering Troy, is forced to stop and resupply his ship on the Island of the Cyclops, ferocious one eyed giants. Odysseus, with a dozen of his best men wandered into the cave of the cyclops Polyphemus, son of Poseidon the god of the seas. Polyphemus, not a believer in the laws of hospitality, eats two of Odysseus' men and traps the rest in his cavern. The ever resourceful Odysseus concocts a plan. With wine from the ship they trick Polyphemus into drunkenness and blind him while he sleeps. Odysseus and his crew escape to the ship and set sail. As the ship pulls away from the Island, Odysseus, unable to resist, boasts to Polyphemus that it was Odysseus, son of Laertes, who had bested him. Polyphemus prays to his father Poseidon for revenge. In turn, Poseidon caused Odysseus to suffer ten more years of trial and hardship. I could only wonder what new ordeals we would encounter, and just what gods we pissed off.

The trip was long and tedious with one brief stop on Okinawa. We then landed in Vietnam at the Army's Americal Division area of operation. Here we spent a day or two acclimating. Our reception by some of their troops was less than hospitable. They attempted to harass us, unaware that most of us were returning vets and were not in the mood for a hassle. Several fights broke out and the hazing abruptly ended.

We had arrived mid morning and were briefed by some of the Americal senior N.C.O.s about conditions on the ground later that afternoon and the next day. The third day the Company moved by a truck convoy to a small village near a fair size river that was to be our base of operation. The C.O. had found nicely elevated ground with open fields. We dug in our perimeter and we were back in the game. Exactly what our mission was, I'm not sure. The main action during the Tet Offensive was the city of Hue and the Marine Base at Khe Sanh in the North, and Saigon and the Mekong River Delta in the South. We were positioned somewhere in the Central Highlands. Shelby's guess was that we relieved other units that moved out to those areas. We began patrolling the area and on several nights our defenses were probed by enemy fire – just a few random shots to let us know we were not alone.

After a couple of weeks, the Company 1st Sergeant called Shelby, me and three other Buck Sergeants to the Company Command Post. We were informed that we had the option of returning to Fort Bragg since we all had brothers who were in Vietnam. Shelby's brother in fact was there with another Company in the 82nd. This was not true for me and the others. Finally, an Army screw up that worked in our favor. We all looked at each other in shock. Top asked for our decision. In turn they all accepted the trip home. To my surprise, I declined. The others looked at me in dismay; Shelby had a more quizzical expression. They gathered up their gear and boarded a truck back to the Americal Division.

What was I thinking? Not wanting to leave under false pretense? A sense of honor? A sense of shirking my duties? Or was it something a little more troubling? Could I actually like this real life game of Cowboys and Indians? I had no answer, however, the more practical question was who would replace Shelby as Platoon Sergeant? There were only three Buck Sergeants left in the Platoon. I didn't know the thoughts of the others, but I knew I didn't want to be the chief adviser to a rookie 2nd Lieutenant. Being a squad leader was challenging enough. All of us were combat experienced, but none of us were pros. We could in all possibility do the job, but I, like the others, had gotten used to having a Lifer like Max, Sgt. Floyd, Sgt. Johnson and Shelby to guide us. Surely the C. O. had other senior NCOs in the Company he could send over. I'm sure the Lieutenant was thinking the same.

My troubled thoughts that night were interrupted by Charlie making a stronger than usual probe of our defense. Did they know Shelby was gone? After all quieted down, late night or early morning, my turn for guard duty over, I fell asleep. I was startled awake at dawn by a familiar voice, "Jesus Christ, Kelly, I'm gone for one day and you let the place turn into a garbage dump." Shelby had returned.

Why? He said he didn't want his brother, me, and the other numbskulls to screw the war up. His real thoughts, he kept to himself. When he made the decision to return to the Platoon, he hitched a ride with a truck convoy heading our way. The lead truck hit a land mine, disabling the truck and stalling the convoy as they searched for other mines. Shelby decided the convoy was too big a target and walked the rest of the way. He walked seven or eight miles alone through the night.

Two days later the three other beneficiaries of the Army's snafu were unceremoniously shipped back to the Company. The mistake as to who's brothers were where had been straightened out. The last time I saw these three fellows they looked very sheepish and nervous in front of the Company Command Post. Shelby later told me they were transferred to other Companies in the Battalion.

After a few days Shelby came over to me and said "Grab your rifle and some grenades, we are going on a recon." The two of us left the perimeter and walked to a near by village. There we bought some cans of Budweiser and a bottle of Manila Rum from some of the kids hawking their wares. After a bit of haggling we paid the kids and we got the sought after "You number one G.I." That was good. If they said "You number ten G. I.", that meant they felt cheated. This was going to be an interesting recon.

Shelby had spotted a Temple on his walk that was about two or three kilometers up river from the village. We decided to go there by boat. We found a village fisherman and his young son heading that way. When they finally understood our gestures they happily agreed to give us a ride. The deal was we would help them fish in exchange for the ride. We needed no poles or nets. We had grenades.

Grenades act like depth charges. Thrown into the water the concussion kills the fish which then float to the surface. The Villager pointed where he wanted us to throw and then his son dove into the river to collect the stunned prey. After four or five explosions they had harvested more fish in fifteen minutes than they could catch in a week. A short time later we reached our destination and left our new friends. They were smiling and waving with an intermittent shout of "You number one G.I." Two number ones in one morning. We were on a roll.

The temple was perched on a small sloping hill overlooking the river. It was magnificent. The fields up to the temple were open and it was an easy climb to the top. When we crested the hill a well cared for formal garden laid before us. A block stone path with a small bridge over a man made, shallow, rock filled pond, meandered for about forty meters to an open stone courtyard ten meters deep and thirty meters across in front of the temple. Two Monks emerged from the temple and greeted us. They were hospitable but somewhat anxious. After a few smiles and bows by all parties the Monks relaxed and gestured for us to explore on our own. The structure was about thirty meters in length with six stone steps approximately fifteen meters long centered on bright red double doors about four meters wide and three meters high and encased in gold trim around the frame.

The roof had two tiers. The second tier was about half the size of the main roof and was raised about one meter above it. The corners of both tiers point up with six foot wood extensions protruding, resembling the curved bow of Viking long boats. The roofing material was like the red clay tiles one would see on a Spanish style house and decorative apple green tiles trimmed the edge. Two large, square columns support the front roof with a matching pair in the back. The columns are light tan with a wide, inlaid dull red stripe, patina shaded symbols are embedded every six inches with twenty markings total on all four sides.

Shelby and I crossed the threshold to be immediately under the gaze of the purpose of the Pagoda, a place of contemplation of the teachings of Buddha. Buddha was sitting on a three meter high platform in an inset on the far, back wall. The inset was at least three meters wide and four meters deep. The approach to the statue consisted of a large center hall, approximately ten by fifteen meters with side entrances left and right. Unlike most Christian churches there were no pews. The Buddha, painted in what looked like bright gold leaf, was about three meters high and two meters wide. Two marble columns flanked Buddha and supported an overhang above the statues head.

Several feet in front of the shrine stood an alter laden with vases of flowers and a plate of fruit piled in pyramid form. On the side walls were several murals of human figures dressed in traditional robes. All of their heads had the background outline of halos as you would see surrounding the heads of saints in a Catholic church. I guess the Buddhists have saints too. On the front walls adjacent to the main entrance there were shelves stacked with urns evidently containing the ashes of cremated ancestors. Many of the urns had photos of the demised inhabitants attached to them.

The center of the hall housed a large glazed, sand filled pot perched on a pedestal base. Poked into the sand was slow burning incense sticks similar to Fourth of July sparklers. The pot also contained scroll like objects that were mostly red in color with what looked like hieroglyphics imprinted on them, possibly some sort of prayer offering.

The floor had the look of polished tile with alternating reddish and dark gray foot size squares. The decorated load-bearing center beam had six telephone pole size columns that looked like red marble evenly spaced supporting it. Standing sentry in the hall were two life size lions matched in stature by two dragons. Since I never saw a dragon, I can not vouch if they were life size or not. There were also two eight foot crane like birds. I began to wonder who built this beautiful structure seemingly in the middle of nowhere and when? Maybe to my mind it was the middle of nowhere because this was not what I was accustomed to. After over fourteen months in Vietnam I realized there was much more to learn and wonder at than just how to survive.

After about an hour of exploring the structure and grounds we bid farewell to the Monks and made our way back to the river. The sun, the rum, and the beer began to take effect as we wandered aimlessly along the river bank. We were traveling away from our Company's position. After a short while we were startled back to sobriety by the rustling of elephant grass on the opposite bank. We quickly took stock of our situation and got into a prone firing position. Our inventory consisted of two M-16s with three magazines of bullets, one grenade left over from our fishing trip, a half bottle of rum and two warm cans of Budweiser. The tension abated when we realized whoever was over there was making far too much noise to be NVA or VC. Sure enough, a rather large body broke through the grass and stepped onto a sandbar that was stretching from the shallow embankment. As the new arrival warily surveyed his surroundings Shelby shouted out, "Hey G.I., want a beer?" Caught completely by surprise, the G. I. dropped to one knee and looked for a place to fire. Shelby again called out, "Look dumb ass, do you want a beer or don't you?" A very relieved reply of "Hell yeah!" came back.

With that Shelby and I stood up and the rest of the Patrol of our newly acquired friend lined up on the opposite shore. At this point the river was about 30 meters wide. Our new acquaintance jumped in and swam over to collect his prize. He guzzled down the beer and assured us that he "had never enjoyed a warm beer more in his life." After a few exchanges of who we were and what we were doing – he was on patrol, we were sightseeing – I realized he was with HQ Company, the same Company as my home town friend Mike Pfeifer. I asked if he knew Sgt. Pfeifer. After a short, startled pause, a big grin stretched over his face "Only a friend of Pfeifer's would be crazy enough to be wandering around half drunk in Indian country. Yeah, I know him!" "Good," I replied, "then give him this and tell him he owes me one when I see him back at Bragg." I handed over our last beer and he swam back to his Patrol. Shelby and I decided to head back to our company perimeter. The recon was over.

I think we must not enter the fight, a man cannot fight on
when he is wounded.

King Nestor, *THE ILIAD*

Several uneventful weeks passed by. There seemed to be a lull in the action by early April. North Vietnamese and Viet Cong Forces had been badly mauled and the thrust of the Tet offense had been blunted. The Marines at Khe Sanh were still under enemy pressure but it did not seem possible that the NVA would be able to take the base. My squad had been assigned a routine patrol and Shelby, as he often did, decided to lead the excursion. The eight of us were moving through some chest high elephant grass. The muddy ground pulling at our boots, slowing progress. After about twenty five meters the point man noticed a slight stream of smoke rising from what looked like a small clearing. As he turned around to signal us of what he suspected shots rang out and a grenade came hurling over the grass towards Shelby and me. At first I thought my cat like reflexes had allowed me to jump out of the way of the explosion. After seeing the blood splotches on my shoulder and leg, I knew I was wrong. I had been hit. Then Shelby whispered, "Hey, Kelly, I think I'm hit." I weakly replied, "Me too." The deadly effect of the mini bomb had luckily been suppressed by landing in the ankle deep mud. The squad fired into the direction of the clearing but no fire was returned. Charlie had left the building.

Another of Max's rules of survival: "Spread out, or one round will get us all." We were not spread out far enough. Fortunately no one else was hit. Shelby and I were medevaced back to an aid station. On the Chopper flight it became apparent to us that our wounds were minor at worst. Shelby thought this was a sign from God, deciding he would go home if given the chance this time. I readily agreed. The Buddhist Monk who read our auras on my first tour came to mind. The prediction of me being slightly wounded came to be. I hoped their pronunciation of Max's battlefield immortality would also hold up.

From the distraught look on the face of the Battalion Chaplain we must have been among the first casualties from the 82nd. After receiving several Blessings and Prayers from the Chaplain we finally convinced him we were O.K. He need not worry, his expertise on the Last Rites would not be tested this day.

The Surgeons began poking and probing for shrapnel fragments from our shoulders, legs and arms. They got some but not all of the metal pieces. I was relieved when the doctors finally stopped. Their surges into my body parts were far more painful than the actual wounds. We were left with rather large scars, our "Red Badge of Courage", where we had been cut to remove the fragments. The Surgeons greatly exaggerated our puny wounds but their efforts made for a better story.

In war there are three bad things that can happen to a soldier: be killed, wounded, or captured. While I have seen the two former, and heard of the latter, you always think it will happen to the other guy. Even though my injuries were relatively trivial, it finally dawned on me that I was the other guy's other guy.

Later that day an officer told us we would be going back to the States for rehab. Shelby would go the hospital at Bragg and I would be sent to Valley Forge Army Hospital in Pennsylvania. These locations were as close to our homes and families as they could get us. I always appreciated the thoughtfulness of the Army in this matter.

My family, of course, was notified of my injuries. The telegram indicated that my injuries were not serious. My Mother could not help but wonder and worry about what the Army thought was not serious. Her apprehensions were quickly relieved when my family came for their first visit to the hospital soon after receiving the initial telegram. I was sitting in a chair in my light blue hospital robe looking tanned, rested and relaxed.

Valley Forge didn't have the same amenities as Camp Zama in Japan where I had spent my Malaria days but the food was passable, I had weekend passes, plus a week furlough. Visitors were the highlight of any given day. Allen Richmond came by with his new girl friend, Lauren. I especially looked forward to visits from a girl I had met on a blind date just prior to my redeployment. Claire was tall and slender with large blue eyes and a friendly and animated face. She was elegant and beautiful. Perhaps Allen and I were both moving on to new phases in our lives.

CHAPTER V

The Devils in Baggy Pants

After my 45 day combination rehabilitation and vacation I was assigned to my third unit in the 82nd, counting the 1st Cavalry, this was my fourth battalion in two and one half years. A far different experience than that of my father and uncles who served with their various regiments from basic training to the end of World War II four years later. True, as the war took it toll many faces changed with replacements. However, the core unit remained intact. I consistently felt like the new kid in school. The 504th earned the nickname "The Devils In Baggy Pants" during the Battle of Anzio in WW II. A diary entry taken from a dead German Officer read, "American Parachutists... devils in baggy pants...are less than 100 meters from my outpost line. I can't sleep at night, they pop up from nowhere and we never know when or where they will strike next. Seems like the black hearted devils are everywhere." I had never thought of myself as a "Black Hearted Devil" before but I kind of liked it. I met up with two friends who had not been redeployed to Vietnam. They needed a third roommate to share expenses for a house they rented off base. I immediately accepted the opportunity. The house was out in the country, about five miles off base. A modern three bedroom, two bath ranch style home on about half an acre of land. This was paradise. No more barracks living with 150 other guys sharing a shower room and the rec room. We still ate at the Mess Hall, the meals were better than our cooking.

Jesse, Dean and I all had between four and six months of service left and were determined to live as normally as possible. Our T.V. got all four stations. We would frequently have parties and barbecues on the weekends. Contrary to what you might think, there were enough young ladies around to keep the events somewhat civilized, not too different from fraternity parties I had attended. We kept the numbers small and occasionally invited the few neighbors we had.

The T.V. was a link to the world outside of our insulated Army existence. Soldiers were aware of the big events of the day such as the riots in 1967 in Newark, Detroit, Watts and even in Plainfield which neighbored my home town. We had newspapers but the Television camera gave a moving form to the unfolding drama. The war was still center stage. We could now hear Walter Cronkite pronounce the war "unwinable".

Mr. Cronkite's assessment did not correspond with the experience of most combat troops at the time. NVA and VC strikes during the Lunar New Year, the most important holiday in Vietnam known as Tet Nguyen Dan or more commonly Tet, were initially successful. The offensive caught the U. S. and AVRN forces by surprise. In years past Tet had been an undeclared, but mutually understood three days of truce. The U. S. Embassy compound in Saigon was penetrated, they laid siege to Khe Sanh, and captured the city of Hue where they murdered over 5,000 civilians deemed to be undesirable; teachers, city officials, anyone they considered to be anti socialist.

However, the general uprising of the population "Uncle Ho" had expected did not happen. My guess is that most folks were a little nervous as to where they stood on the "sufficiently socialist" scale. All of the VC who entered the U. S. Embassy compound were killed. The siege of Khe San was broken and Hue was retaken in a matter of weeks. About 50,000 V.C. alone were killed, and what remaining forces the V.C. had would not play a significant role in the conflict again. The NVA itself would not be able to launch a major offensive again and they retreated to their sanctuaries in Cambodia and Laos. Allowing the enemy a safe haven may make sense to a politician, but certainly not to a soldier.

On February 27th, 1968, reporting from Vietnam, Mr. Cronkite said:

> *"Tonight, back in more familiar surroundings in New York, we'd like to sum up our findings in Vietnam, an analysis that must be speculative, personal, subjective. Who won and who lost in the great Tet offensive against the cities? I'm not sure. The Vietcong did not win by a knockout, but neither did we. The referees of history may make it a draw. Another standoff may be coming in the big battles expected south of the Demilitarized Zone. Khe Sanh could well fall, with a terrible loss in American lives, prestige and morale, and this is a tragedy of our stubbornness there; but the bastion no longer is a key to the rest of the northern regions, and it is doubtful that the American forces can be defeated across the breadth of the DMZ with any substantial loss of ground. Another standoff. On the political front, past performance gives no confidence that the Vietnamese government can cope with its problems, now compounded by the attack on the cities. It may not fall, it may hold on, but it probably won't show the dynamic qualities demanded of this young nation. Another standoff.*
>
> *We have been too often disappointed by the optimism of the American leaders, both in Vietnam and Washington, to have faith any longer in the silver linings they find in the darkest clouds. They may be right, that Hanoi's winter-spring offensive has been forced by the Communist realization that they could not win the longer war of attrition, and that the Communists hope that any success in the offensive will improve their position for eventual negotiations. It would improve their position, and it would also require our realization, that we should have had all along, that any negotiations must be that - negotiations, not the dictation of peace terms. For it seems now more certain than ever that the bloody experience of Vietnam is to end in a stalemate. This summer's almost certain standoff will either end in real give-and-take negotiations or terrible escalation; and for every means we*

have to escalate, the enemy can match us, and that applies to invasion of the North, the use of nuclear weapons, or the mere commitment of one hundred, or two hundred, or three hundred thousand more American troops to the battle. And with each escalation, the world comes closer to the brink of cosmic disaster.

To say that we are closer to victory today is to believe, in the face of the evidence, the optimists who have been wrong in the past. To suggest that we are on the edge of defeat is to yield to unreasonable pessimism. To say that we are mired in stalemate seems the only realistic, yet unsatisfactory, conclusion. On the off chance that military and political analysts are right, in the next few months we must test the enemy's intentions, in case this is indeed his last big gasp before negotiations. But it is increasingly clear to this reporter that the only rational way out then will be to negotiate, not as victors, but as an honorable people who lived up to their pledge to defend democracy, and did the best they could."

Some time after that broadcast, President Johnson is reported to have said, "If I have lost Cronkite, I've lost middle America." Johnson later decided not to seek reelection. Mr. Cronkite's assessment became the political turning point that Ho Chi Minh and Giap needed. It gave credibility to the anti-war movement and now men will die to preserve a tie.

❖   ❖   ❖

It was late June of 1968. Senior and Junior Non Coms with combat experience from the 504ˢᵗ were selected for an assignment to train ROTC recruits coming to Fort Bragg for two weeks. The core agenda; land navigation, fire and maneuver, and patrolling techniques. For the better part of the summer, up until mid August, we rotated through different groups of students from various colleges and universities in the South.

The key word in ROTC is "Officer". These are guys my age who will become leaders of infantry platoons and companies in the near future. Most of what they knew about these matters came from the Army Training Manual. We, the trainers, saw it as our duty to add the more practical application to the "Book" and were diligent in imparting our experience to the trainees.

This had an interesting effect on me. I began wondering if I was becoming a professional soldier. Things I thought of as common knowledge were entirely new to these college students. I thought of Sergeants Floyd, Maxwell, Shelby, Jackson and other Non Coms who led us so ably. Could I be one of them? Officers Candidate School was still an option. Suddenly a life in the Army became a possibility. My discharge date of the 15th of November, 1968 was fast approaching. First Sergeant Merrick offered a promotion to Staff Sergeant E-6, providing I passed the required test, if I would enlist for another three years. Company Commander Howell's recommendation also for O. C. S. ultimately was not sufficient influence to pull me away from my perception of freedom in civilian life. Just as an acolyte leaves the seminary before ordination, I decided God had not given me a military calling. My odyssey remained shrouded in a fog.

BOOK II

WAS ANYBODY THINKING?

CHAPTER VI

Ye Olde College Try

Part II

Discharged at last, I went back home to New Jersey. Back home to the room I shared with my brother. Back home to the house where my father built the second story. Back to my little sister who loved when my friends came over. Back to a bed without a mosquito net dangling over it. That summer the 82nd also discharged Mike Pfeifer upon his return from Vietnam. Attempting to adjust to civilian life, Mike and I caused our parents many sleepless nights.

While enjoying a beer at our favorite watering hole, The Somerset Tavern, some friends asked us if we would go with them to a music festival in New York, Woodstock was the town. With the exception of Janis Joplin, the names of the performers were only vaguely familiar to me. No Smokey and The Miracles, no Temptations, but it sounded like fun. The only problem: no hotel. They were just camping out under the upstate sky, that killed the deal. "Camping out" had lost its charm for us. We wouldn't have gone even if The Miracles were playing.

Another night, another bar with one of those Irish Pub sounding names: O'Sullivan's or Shaunessy's. There were usually more girls at those places. We ran into two girls who were friends of friends. We didn't know them very well, but at closing time they lured us back to their apartment with promises of more beer. It was an old Victorian style house. Their apartment was on the second floor. Armed with a six pack, we climbed out onto a wide ledge to watch the sun come up. Mike casually mentioned that we were ex-paratroopers. The girls were skeptical, maybe we didn't look very tough, or coordinated, after drinking a half case of beer each. To prove Mike's point, I jumped off the ledge. Immediately I realized this was not a good idea, but having consumed enough beer I was relaxed and executed an excellent three point hit, shift and rotate landing. Then again if I had not drunk so much beer I probably would not have been foolish enough to jump in the first place. The girls were shocked, Mike, however, gave the jump an eight out of a possible ten points. He felt I was a little out of practice. The sun rose, then Mike and I headed for home. As I limped to the car Mike quipped, "Maybe our parents should worry!"

In between the late nights, a family friend lined me up with a union job at the New Jersey Power and Light Company. After taking a battery of tests to evaluate my mechanical abilities, I was assigned to an underground crew. There my talents for digging holes and breaking things, mostly concrete, were best utilized. It was obvious I wasn't going to earn a living as a skilled electrical lineman. This heightened my resolve to return to college. The pay was decent with benefits, vacation time and no weekend work. I could endure digging holes for a year.

I applied to several schools, mostly in the south. Even paying out of state tuition southern schools were more affordable than the New Jersey state schools. When stationed at Bragg my housemate Jesse and I spent several weekend passes visiting his hometown of Princeton, Kentucky near the home of the 101st Airborne Division at Fort Campbell. Princeton, the proverbial rural one stop light town is the seat of Caldwell County. Out of Kentucky's one hundred nineteen counties one hundred of them were dry. Caldwell fit among the majority. However, Jesse had credit with the local bootlegger, access to beer was never a problem. It always seemed somewhat odd that most of the bourbon whiskey produced in the state could not be purchased in its originating county. Close by is a great recreational area, The Land Between The Lakes. Damming the Tennessee River formed the Kentucky and Barkley Lakes. Jesse's large family had several boats and we spent many lazy days enjoying the leech free water. He and I began our post 82nd Airborne lives on the same day. Immediately Jesse returned to Princeton. He said he wouldn't get rich there, but he could lead a good life.

I loved the laid back attitude of the people I met there. My excitement ran high when Western Kentucky University accepted me as a student for the Fall Semester. On academic probation of course, due to my less than stellar performance previously.

Late August of 1969 I packed my one suitcase and drove my Firebird west through Pennsylvania to Columbus, Ohio and then headed south on Interstate 71 towards Cincinnati; across the Ohio River and into my new home of Kentucky. My route avoided the Appalachian Mountains and coal fields of Eastern Kentucky, and took me to the heart of the bluegrass country. Bluegrass, which has green leaves, derives its name from its blue flower when the grass grows to its natural height of two or three feet. The name Kentucky means meadow lands in several native dialects. The savannah that supported bison in days gone by were now dotted with picturesque thoroughbred horse farms with miles of crisp white post and slat fencing with neatly trimmed barns and stalls. Many people view New Jersey from the Turnpike connecting Philadelphia and New York City. They pass through the heart of the industrial area of New Jersey and think that is all that there is. However, the hills of Somerset County and the flat lands of Monmouth County have horse farms not too different than Kentucky, minus the bluegrass. Louisville and Lexington, with populations of 500,000 and 250,000 dominate the bluegrass region. The western third of the state is more rural with small towns such as Princeton. Instead of horse farms, soybean and tobacco farms are the norm.

WKU is a fairly large public university of about 13,000 students, mostly Kentuckians, but with a smattering of northerners to keep it interesting. Western had excellent athletic programs in football and track, and they were a national power in basketball. While I no longer had any motivation or desire to compete in sports, it provided good entertainment on weekends. Academically, as my student adviser put it, "a third of our students would fair well in the Ivy League, for a third this is exactly the right environment, and a third don't belong in college at all." My determination was not to fall amongst the latter, again.

Western is in Bowling Green with a population around 50,000 lying 55 miles north of Nashville, Tennessee and 120 miles south of Louisville. During the Civil War Bowling Green was declared the Confederate Capital of Kentucky. Contrastingly, Louisville, the largest city in Kentucky, was the southern most Northern city. While most of Kentucky sided with the North, it was hard to find a Kentuckian who would admit this. Most like to think their ancestors were rebels. At least the white citizens did. Perhaps the fact that both Abraham Lincoln and Jefferson Davis were born 100 miles, and one year apart in Kentucky, explains the confusion in my newly adopted state.

Returning to college at this period would prove to be interesting. The anti-war movement was gaining momentum and Richard M. Nixon was elected President with a secret plan to honorably extract the U.S. from Vietnam.

My transition from the Army to a job and then back to college in less than a year evolved smoothly. I decided against living in one of the University dormitories. I did not want a roommate and chose a sleeping room at a large private house, walking distance from campus. The room was on the second floor, had a separate entrance from the owner's quarters and was furnished with a bed, a desk set and a windsor back chair. The money I saved from breaking concrete, along with the monthly stipend awarded to all Vietnam Veterans enrolled in college, meant I would not have to work. At least not for the first semester.

The semester went well, I began making friends in classes and found there were at least fifty veterans on campus. I suspected that number would grow greatly in the coming years. I managed to control my impulse to socialize and focused on the task at hand: studying and grades. I finished the Fall semester with three A's, one B and to no surprise a C in math for non math majors. As a History major, only the looming required statistics course remained to be vanquished. Highlighting my sense of achievement, my faculty advisor recommended I be removed from academic probation. Then the coup de grace, my application to be considered an in state student was accepted. My tuition would now be three hundred dollars a year. Although my cash savings had expired, a part time job at McDonalds would easily fill the gap. All in all not a bad start to a new year.

Spring of 1970 also went well. I began to realize I didn't have to continue my hermit-like existence to maintain good grades. Luckily, Bowling Green was not in a dry county and I began taking advantage of the social life the University and town offered. Frat parties, house parties, the local bars, concerts and ball games began to fill my calendar, confined mostly to weekends of course. I replaced my job at McDonalds with a bartending position at a college hangout called the Hilltopper Pub.

As the summer approached, I decided to remain in Bowling Green. I would take classes during the Summer Semester and continue my job at the Hilltopper Pub insuring my employment for the Fall. I spent a few weekends visiting Claire in New Jersey and she came to Kentucky a few times before returning to her classes.

Two friends and I rented a house in a subdivision near Bowling Green. Aaron Adams had served with the 75th Ranger Regiment in Vietnam and Ray Roberts had served his time with a mountain division in Alaska. We found a brick ranch house with three bedrooms, no garage but enough parking for our cars. The importance of brick loomed large in Aaron's house hunting requirements. Why this was imperative remained a mystery to Ray and me. It was self evident to one Kentucky native, and he viewed explaining the significance to a couple of dunder heads as a waste of time. The story of The Three Little Pigs must have been told with greater fervor in the south. Brick domicile acquired, we assigned the bedrooms by rank. Ray, a 2nd Lieutenant had first pick; Aaron, a Staff Sergeant picked second; and I, a lowly Buck Sergeant got the brightly colored child's room with a clown face for the light switch. Not exactly the lair of a grizzled warrior.

Like many veterans on campus, Aaron was in his second round at college. He attended Western on a football scholarship before being drafted. I suspected he shared my focus problem as well. We all called him Big A, at 6'5" and 270 pounds, the name fit. Eventually everyone in our expanding circle was called "Big" something; Big Dave, Big Ken. This ceremonious nicknaming was a Kentucky tradition that denoted friendship and comradery. Though we did refrain from calling the girls "Big" ...Big Alice, Big Mary. We weren't sure they would understand the spirit of friendship.

The Summer sun began to dim and the Fall semester commenced. After my successful first year I was confident I would be able to handle the rigors of academia. Aaron, Ray and I quickly fell into the routine of classes and, like most veterans on campus, we all had jobs but managed to find some time to throw parties on the weekend. Our house became party central. As the semester progressed I missed a class or two due to my occasionally late hours working at the pub. Slowly the weekends began to start on Thursday night instead of Friday. Studying and reviewing class material nightly transformed to pulling all nighters and cramming for tests. When final grades were posted my A's and B's from last year were B's and C's. I barely eked out a D in statistics. Here at Western there was no First Sergeant or Battalion Commander to haul me back in line. If I wanted to succeed, the discipline would have to come from within. My mission for the next semester became obvious. I once again trusted the map and compass readings; attend all classes, study every night, and the weekend began on Friday evening.

For Spring break, instead of making a ritual trip to Florida I decided to visit Claire at UConn. Tribal behavior is not reserved for the far reaches of distant lands. A visit to the UConn Student Union gave me a front row seat. Claire's sorority was conducting a campaign recruiting volunteers to help make minor painting and property improvements for elderly residents in the housing projects of Hartford. At their table they had leaflets and were collecting names and phone numbers from interested students. Diane, the sorority president, noticed another group with a similar mission. She approached them to see if working together would create a synergy. The other group was representative of the hippies on campus. I observed from a distance and wondered if this cross pollination of cultures could take hold? The sorority girls with their neatly styled hair and preppy clothing and the non-conforming hippies in their frayed jeans and granny glasses. Even in nonconformity, there is a need to conform with the peer group with which you identify. Every tribe must have their code and uniform. Diane was coldly rebuffed. Obviously, anyone who belonged to a sorority couldn't possibly have a sincere concern for the less fortunate, much less have any ideas on how to help others. No alliance would be formed. The tribes would go their separate ways.

That evening we were at a local pub with a variety of Claire's friends and acquaintances. The conversation touched on the day's encounter with the hippies, plans for their trip to Hartford and other topics both great and small. The 1970's budding environmental movement had prompted some in our group to read Rachel Carson's SILENT SPRING and THE POPULATION BOMB by Paul Ehrlich. We divided between true believers in the coming disasters and the skeptics. Claire and I were among the latter. Dr. Ehrlich's basic premise is that population growth is outpacing human ability to feed everyone, therefore forced population control is necessary. My problem has been who gets to decide how the control is applied? Ehrlich, and people like him, believe only in the tangible resources they can see and touch and do not allow for the God given resources of the mind, spirit and ingenuity of man to adapt and overcome the limitations of the material world. In my mind the food issues were more a matter of distribution and political policies, not an agricultural issue. He who controls the food or medicine or energy for that matter, controls the people. This issue proved to be an entertaining topic of discussion. To bolster my assertion of food as a means of control, I gave the example of Joseph Stalin in 1932 when he premeditated the starvation of the Ukrainians. The Ukraine, a country under the domination of Czarist Russia and now the Soviet Union, was known as the bread basket of Europe. When the Ukrainians resisted Stalin's five year plan and the collectivization of farms in 1932, Stalin seized all grain and land and allowed no shipment of other food stuffs into the Ukraine. By the end of 1933 about 25 percent of the region's population, including three million children, had starved to death. Debate about the death penalty proved to be a little more contentious. I didn't start the conversation and always had mixed feelings on the subject. I had researched the subject for a paper and in this evening's discussion argued that the death penalty is not a determent to crime and we do not have the right to kill. We had all probably had too many beers when one of the girls, Gail, blurted out "But didn't you kill people in Vietnam?" I chose to overlook her ignorant challenge and took it as a sign that I was winning the debate. Claire, on the other hand, scorched Gail with the anger in her gaze. Gail quickly offered an awkward apology and the conversation turned to lighter topics. I realized the girl I had fallen in love with was not only bright and beautiful, but fiercely protective and not afraid to stand her ground. Many of my high school friends were now starting careers and getting married. This was the first time such a notion entered my consciousness. I thought

Claire and I could have a good life together, but not yet.

CHAPTER VII

La Rue Sans Joie

Press him yourself to tell the whole truth.
He'll never lie – the man is far too wise

ATHENA, *THE ODYSSEY*

It had been over three years since I left the highland jungles, valleys and rice paddies. In comparison, life at Western was stress free, not even statistics could unnerve me. Odysseus lingered on his journey home for seven years as the captive and lover of the beautiful goddess Calypso on her island. Eventually her promise of immortality could not keep him from once again confronting the wrath of Poseidon as he set sail for Ithaca and home. While I had no plans for immortality and no vengeful god to face, spending two more years on this island oasis of Kentucky seemed about right. The Vietnam War, however, would keep intruding into my idyllic existence.

Big A and I, as with most of the Vets, didn't share much of our Vietnam experience with each other, there was no need. The dates and the places change, but the stress, fear, courage and cowardice are universal. Telling war stories to a bunch of college kids didn't seem appropriate either. For the most part, we didn't think they wanted to hear them anyway.

An ever popular refrain and bumper sticker of the peace movement is "Make love, not war." Since the human population is approaching four billion and the history of mankind even before the Bronze Age was replete with warfare, it would appear that humanity has an infinite capacity for both. It was likely the Vietnam War would be the only direct involvement I would have in a military conflict. As a budding historian, I thought I would learn as much about it as possible.

Military training and practical experience taught me what to expect from the Vietcong and the North Vietnamese soldiers. They were tough, resourceful, enduring and ruthless. Most of my encounters were with various units of the NVA regulars. After the 1968 TET Offensive, it was particularly clear that the war was fueled by the Communist North. The Vietcong Rebels did not have the strength or local support to overthrow the South Vietnamese government. I had only a vague understanding of the French involvement prior to that of the United States. I knew the Geneva Convention of 1954 divided the country into two parts and independence from France was achieved. So why did Ho Chi Mich and Vu Nguyen Giap deem it necessary to rule the South as well as the North? Just who are these two characters? How did France come to rule Vietnam? How and why did the U. S. get involved?

I began to research this subject and soon discovered Dr Bernard B. Fall in the tomes of Western's library. Dr. Fall wrote seven books and numerous articles regarding the first Indo-China War from 1946 – 1954. The two I chose to read were STREET WITHOUT JOY and HELL IN A VERY SMALL PLACE.

A soldier, scholar, war correspondent, and an expert on Indochina (Vietnam, Laos and Cambodia), Dr. Fall's life was filled with accomplishment and adventure. As a teenager he fought with the French underground against the German occupation. In 1951 he came to the United States and earned his Masters and Doctorate Degrees at Syracuse University. He was an Assistant Professor at American University and in 1956 he began teaching International Relations at Howard University.

Western Europe's first influential contact with this region came during the great world exploratory period of the 16th century. Mission-aries and traders mostly from Portugal and France seemed to travel the world together and eventually established a post in Vietnam. By the year 1700 about a tenth of the Vietnamese population had converted to Christianity. From the early 1600's Vietnam was controlled by two very powerful families, the Nguyens in the south and the Trinhs in the north. Not surprisingly, the territory was divided roughly at the same parallel as now. Not much in history seems to change; not human nature, not disputes over territory, nor control over our fellow men. Technology is the lone variable.

In 1788 a French missionary, Bishop Pigneaux de Behaine, came to the aid of the Nguyens during an internal Vietnamese conflict. The Bishop raised an army of 3,000 men from the French territory of PonDicherry in India. With the Bishop's help, Nguyen Anh, the patriarch of the family, defeated his opponents and became Emperor in 1792. As a concession, Christianity would be tolerated and trade with France began to flourish under Nguyen Anh. Things began to change under the next Emperor, Minh Mang, whose reign began in 1820. Minh Mang and the next two Emperors were devout Confucians and viewed Christianity and the West as threats. Suppression and persecu-tion of Catholics began and trade slowed. This gave Napoleon III the excuse to invade Vietnam in order to protect French interests. From 1858 to 1893 the French slowly, in spite of many revolts, gained control of most of Vietnam and Indochina. Su Tzu, the 5th century Chinese au-thor of THE ART OF WAR said, "We cannot enter into alliances until we are acquainted with the designs of our neighbors." The Nguyens did not examine the motives of their French allies closely enough.

The end of World War I brought about many changes, both polit-ical and economic. The maps of Europe and the mideast were redrawn. Japan evolved from a feudal state to a modern industrial and military power. In 1905 the Japanese Navy defeated the Russian Navy, the first major defeat of a Western power by East Asian forces since the time of Genghis Khan in the 13th century.

In Vietnam a new figure emerged, Nguyen Sinh Cung, his father was a Confucian scholar and a local magistrate. Nguyen received his education at a French school in the former imperial capital city of Viet-nam during the Nguyen dynasty, Hue. After his schooling he traveled and worked in the United States and England. At the end of World War I, he moved to France. Always an anti-colonialist, he petitioned President Wilson to help remove the French from Vietnam, but was ignored. In the early 1920s Nguyen visited the Marxist/Leninist Russia where his willing indoctrination of communist principles took hold. In 1924 he returned to Paris and became a founder of the French Communist Party (Parti Communiste Francais). The outbreak of World War II gave Nguyen, now known as Ho Chi Minh (He Who Enlightens), the opportunity he needed to try freeing Vietnam from the French.

The French defeat by Germany led to a puppet government known as Vichy France. The Vichy administration also included French colonies like Vietnam. In 1941 Ho Chi Minh returned to his homeland which was now occupied by Germany's ally, Japan. Ho became the leader of the resistance movement, the Viet Minh, an abbreviation for "League for the Independence of Vietnam".

The efforts of Ho Chi Minh and the Viet Minh were supported by the American Office of Strategic Services (OSS), the forerunner of the CIA. On September 2, 1945, after the final defeat of Japan, Ho Chi Minh declared Vietnam independent. Vietnam's ancient nemesis, China, under the leadership of Generalissimo Chiang Kai-Shek, sent 200,000 troops to occupy Hanoi. This action forced "Uncle Ho", as G.I.s referred to him, into forming a coalition with the French to force out the Chinese. As Uncle Ho said, "The last time the Chinese came, they stayed a thousand years. The French and foreigners, they are weak. Colonialism is dying. The white man is finished in Asia. But if the Chinese stay now, they will never go. As for me I prefer to sniff French shit for five years, than to eat Chinese shit for the rest of my life."

By the end of 1946 after diplomatic failure with the French, it became clear to Ho Chi Minh that the French would not allow an independent and autonomous state of Vietnam. Therefore, he declared war.

Now that the stage had been set, Dr. Fall began to chronicle the combatants, battles, strategies and events in his book STREET WITHOUT JOY. The title of the book comes from the main highway along the coast of Vietnam simply called Road #1. The French Union Troops christened it "LaRue Sons Joie" due to the many battles and hardships they suffered there. The French Union Forces were comprised of the legendary Foreign Legion; Regular French Units; Vietnamese, mostly from the southern provinces; Cambodians; Laotians; Algerians; Moroccans and Sengalese.

The Viet Minh military brains and commander Nguyen Vo Giap was a graduate of Hanoi University with degrees in economics, history and politics. Giap studied the military history and philosophy of Napoleon Bonaparte and Sun Tzu.

There were other nationalist groups in Vietnam, many which did not want Communist rule any more than French, but the relatively well armed and organized Viet Minh killed or terrorized these factions into submission. I could sense Dr. Fall's frustration with the French government when he observed "the French managed to lose the second round – that of political negotiations – through their own stubbornness and their unwillingness to see the situation as it was: they had been defeated, through their own fault and that of their allies; and they did not have the overwhelming military force needed to make a military test of strength between themselves and the Viet Minh which would be so obviously hopeless for the latter that they would not attempt it. And France, in 1946, seemed a likely bet for Communist domination herself. The French forces sent to Indochina were too strong for France to resist the temptation of using them; yet not strong enough to keep the Viet Minh from trying to solve the whole political problem by throwing the French into the sea. The outbreak of the Indochina War can be retraced back to that single tragic erroneous estimate."

The war almost ended in October, 1947 when 1,137 paratroopers from Airborne Group "S" landed and surprised the Viet Minh Headquarters, almost capturing Ho Chi Minh and General Giap and other senior leaders. Failing to cut the head of the snake, the conflict dragged on for eight more years.

After a few more losses to the French forces, which were better equipped with conventional arms and technologically superior, General Giap returned to the ancient tactics which had helped the Vietnamese defeat Kubla Kahn's unbeatable Mongols in the late 13th century. Simply put, the weaker and outnumbered Viets lured the Mongols deep into the jungle – which covers about 50% of the land mass with another 35% forest. Since the time of Genghis Kahn the Mongols had already defeated every European and Moslem army in their path. They were highly organized with superior horse borne archers, extremely mobile cavalry tactics, and the most technically advanced weapons of the day. Their hardened leather armor, along with tightly woven silk shirts could prevent arrows from penetrating their skin. The Mongols rarely, contrary to popular belief, outnumbered their adversaries. The speed and surprise of their movements only made them seem that way. The physical tactic of terror was also a mainstay - surrender your city or all men, women and children will die and die painfully. All of the Mongols advantages, much like French and American tanks and armored vehicles, were useless in the thick jungle lacking room to maneuver. Confined to the few roads that existed, they became prime targets for ambush. Along with the jungle, heat and disease defeated the first Mongol invasion.

Several years later, the Mongols came back with 400 warships, again the Viets outsmarted them and lured the Mongols up the Broh Dang River which runs into the Gulf of Tonkin. The Viets had driven iron stakes into the riverbed, just below the surface of the water. The Mongol ships were impaled. The trapped ships were sunk, captured or burned by flaming arrows launched from the shore. Their use of the iron stakes reminds me of the dreaded pungi pits encountered in the Vietnam War. The V. C. would dig camouflaged holes in the ground and place sharp bamboo stakes dipped in fecal matter. The pungi pits I encountered were relatively small, large enough to entrap a leg with enough stakes to cause severe damage when you attempted to extract your leg from the pit. The enemy viewed a wounded soldier as more damaging than a dead one. A helicopter would have to be called to transport the injured trooper, exposing the chopper to fire and causing the rest of the unit to halt their movement. They would also put barbed spikes in rice paddies and wait for unsuspecting or careless G. I.s to step on them.

Time tested tactics can only work so long against a modern army. Even the victorious Viets of the 13th century had to pay tribute to the Mongols to maintain peace and autonomy. The Mongols were invaders with no ties to Vietnam. The French, on the other hand, had established an ingrained culture as well as a political system, and an economic system within the country. True the Viet-Minh controlled the jungle, but you cannot rule a country from mosquito infested swamps.

In November of 1949 help arrived from an ancient rival of the

Vietnamese but ideological ally of the Viet-Minh. Mao Tse Tung and the communists drove the western friendly regime of Chang Kai Shek out of China. Giap now had a safe haven, a sanctuary on Vietnam's northern border. Here he could train and form his guerrilla forces into a disciplined army with an order of battle. He now had a source for supplies, mortars, and artillery. Most important, Giap had time to plan his strategy for the defeat of the French.

The French, ever in search of a conventional battle with the Viet-Minh, wanted to bring their superior fire power into play and decided on a risky strategy. In November 1954 General Navarre, the commander of the French Union Forces, ordered a parachute drop of his best units into an isolated, nondescript valley called Dien Bien Phu, in English – the Seat of the Border County Administration. Navarre hoped these units would be a tempting target for Giap and the Viet-Minh. The French strategists overestimated their ability and underestimated the resourcefulness of Giap and the Viet-Minh. What the French did not take into account was that they were no longer facing lightly armed and undisciplined guerrillas but a well trained and equipped modern army thanks to their Russian and Chinese allies. At peak, the French forces were comprised of three thousand French Paratroops, three thousand Foreign Legion Airborne Troops, plus Vietnamese and Africans - thirteen thousand total. Giap had fifty thousand combat troops plus fifty thousand support people. The Viet-Minh hauled artillery up the surrounding hills and the fate of the French Garrison at Dien Bien Phu was sealed.

In STREET WITHOUT JOY Dr. Fall relates Giap's plan:

> "Giap outlined the Indochina war as consisting of three stages. First was that of the initial retreat of the Viet-Minh forces until they had time to re-train and consolidate. The second phase would begin when the French, failing to destroy the Viet-Minh guerilla forces, would allow them to re-equip themselves and with the help of the Chinese Communists, to eliminate slowly but surely most of the small French posts in the Viet-Minh base area. The third stage was to be the total destruction of the French troops. In Giap's own words:

> 'The enemy will pass slowly from the offensive to the defen-

sive. The Blitzkrieg will transform itself into a war of long duration. Thus, the enemy will be caught in a dilemma: he has to drag out the war in order to win it and does not possess, on the other hand, the psychological and political means to fight a long drawn-out war.'

Giap was no fool. Being perfectly informed as to the situation of French morale at home and fully aware of Americas' hesitation to commit United States troops in a 'colonial' war, Giap felt it important to liquidate the French as a military threat before the arrival of massive American material aid. Giap stated further:

'Our strategy early in the course of this third stage is that of a general counter offensive. We shall attack without cease until final victory, until we have swept the enemy forces from Indo-china. During the first and second stages, we have gnawed away at the enemy forces; now we must destroy them. All military activities of the third stage must tend to the same simple aim – the total destruction of French forces.

We shall go on to the general counter-offensive when the following conditions will have been fulfilled: (1) superiority of our forces over those of the enemy; (2) the international situation is in our favor; (3) the military situation is in our favor. We will have to receive aid from abroad in order to be able to carry out the counter offensive, but to count solely upon it without taking into account our own capabilities is to show proof of subjectivism and of lack of political conscience. But on the other hand we cannot deny the importance of such aid.

Whenever we have reached the third stage, the following tactical principles will be applied: mobile warfare will become the principal activity, positional warfare and guerrilla warfare will become secondary.' "

Giap laid out his strategy in 1950 and this is the plan used against the United States. I wonder how many of our Generals and politicians read this? It seems Giap was determined to frustrate us as he had the French – fighting longer engagements only at his choosing – otherwise, hit and run and then fade into the jungle.

The French could only supply the Garrison by parachute drops. The Viet Minh tightened the noose around Dien Bien Phu. Near the end, untrained airborne replacements parachuted in. Surprisingly, their casualty rate from the jump was not higher than that from trained paratroopers. Why did we waste all of that time in Jump School? What went through the minds of the doomed soldiers? Surely they knew they were doomed, just like the Texans at the Alamo and the Spartans at Thermopoli. I was thankful I never had to face such a situation.

It appeared the tide could only be turned against the Viet-Minh by American air power. Dr. Fall, in his book HELL IN A VERY SMALL PLACE, THE SIEGE OF DIEN BIEN PHU, poses the question, "Why did France herself not provide her armed forces in Indochina with adequate air force?" Dr. Fall concluded the core answer was, "just as the French had not known how to use their tanks in 1940 against the Germans, they did not know how to use their air force in 1954. A good part of why Dien Bien Phu was lost lies right there." There were other problems; lack of air fields and lack of planes.

Dr. Fall's second question, "Why did the United States, knowing full well what was at stake, fail to provide the lacking air power, after all?" Dr. Fall's answer, "According to his own memoirs, President Eisenhower still felt in January, 1954 that the United States ground forces would not be required in Southeast Asia and that American air strikes in support of the French against communist forces deployed in the jungle would be of little effectiveness and, in his words, "would create a double jeopardy; it would comprise an act of war and would also entail the risk of having intervened and lost."

The President also saw the potential of escalating hostilities and possibly drawing the Communist Chinese into the war with their Russian made jet fighters and bombers, and their huge army now free from commitments in Korea with the signing of that truce. Whatever the American calculations, Giap had guessed right. Although the United States was funding and supplying the French, the Americans would not get directly involved in what could be perceived as a colonial war.

Dr. Fall faithfully, and in great detail depicts the events of the nine year struggle, the battles, the courage of his countrymen, the foreign legionnaires, Vietnamese, Cambodians, Laotians, Algerians, Moroccans, and Sengalese. He writes about the opposition to the war back home, the stoning of returning wounded soldiers by French communists. Dr. Fall was obviously discouraged with the often bumbling and misunderstanding of the nature of the war in Indochina by the French government and high command. Then there is the arrogance the French, on occasion, are known for. Dr. Fall related an observation while in Cambodia near the famous Temple of Angkor-Wat. Safely removed from combat areas, this was more like a resort town. While seated at a table near tennis courts Dr. Fall waited for an officer playing tennis to arrange his transportation to the Cambodian capital of Phnom-Penh.

"Then emerged from the verandah a soldier in French uniform. His small stature, brown skin and western-type features showed him to be a Cambodian. He wore the blue field cap with the golden anchor of the Troupes Coloniales – the French 'Marine' – and the three golden chevrons of a Master-Sergeant. On his chest above the left breast pocket of his suntan regulation shirt were three rows of multi-colored ribbons: croix de guerre with four citations, campaign ribbons with the clasp of France's every colonial campaign since the Moroccan pacification of 1926; the Italian campaign of 1943 and the drive to the Rhine of 1945. In his left hand, he carried several papers crossed diagonally with a tri-colored ribbon; travel orders, like mine, which also awaited the signature of one of the officers.

He remained in the shadow of the verandah's awning until the officers had interrupted their game and had joined the two women with their drinks, then strode over in a measured military step, came stiffly to attention in a military salute, and handed the orders for himself and his squad to the captain. The captain looked up in surprise. Still with a half smile on his face from the remark he had made previously. His eyes narrowed suddenly as he understood that he was being interrupted. Obviously, he was annoyed, but not really furious.

'Sergeant, you can see that I'm busy. Please wait until I have time to deal with your travel orders. Don't worry. You will have them in time for the convoy.'

The sergeant stood stiffly at attention, some of his almost white hair glistening in the sun where it peeked from under the cap, his wizened face betraying no emotion whatever. 'A vous orders, mon capitaine.' A sharp salute, a snappy about face. The incident was closed. The officers had had their drink and now resumed their game.

The sergeant resumed his watch near where the Cambodian messboys were following the game, but this time he had squatted down on his haunches, a favorite Cambodian position of repose which would leave most Europeans with partial paralysis for several hours afterwards.

Almost without moving his head, he attentively followed the tennis game, his travel orders still tightly clenched in his left hand.

The sun began to settle behind the trees of the garden and a slight cooling breeze rose from nearby Lake Tonle-Sap, Cambodia's inland sea. It was 1700(Hrs).

All of a sudden, there rose behind the trees, from the nearby French camp, the beautiful bell-clear sounds of a bugle playing "Lower the Flag" - the signal which, in the French Army, marks the end of the working day as the colors are struck.

Nothing changed at the tennis court, the two officers continued to play their set, the women continued their chatter, and the mess hall boys their silent vigil.

Only the old sergeant had moved. He was now standing stiffly at attention, his right hand raised to the cap in the flat-palmed salute of the French Army, facing in the direction from which the bugle tunes came; saluting as per regulations, France's tricolor hidden behind the trees. The rays of the set-

ting sun shone upon the immobile brown figure, catching the gold of the anchor and of the chevrons and one of the tiny metal stars of his ribbons.

Something very warm welled up in me. I felt like running over to the little Cambodian who had fought all his life for my country, and apologizing to him for my countrymen here who didn't care about him, and for my countrymen in France who didn't even care about their countrymen fighting in Indochina... and in one single blinding flash, I knew that we were going to lose the war."

As I read Dr. Fall's words I had no epiphany about the outcome of our war, only the knowledge that I had behaved like those haughty French officers. Gooks, slope heads, slant eyes, racial slurs we G.I.s used all too frequently when referring to the Vietnamese friend or foe. In some ways we may have given the foe more respect when we called the Viet Cong "Victor Charlie" or simply "Charlie". Victor is the military call letter for V, Charlie is the call letter for C. Demonizing the enemy can be understood, but after reading Dr. Fall's passage I felt remorse for my thoughtless reference to a friend. I recalled an incident while on a six man patrol we caught two farmers by surprise. They were planting rice in terraced paddies. We were going up the hill in our patrol path. As usual it was unbearably hot and humid and we decided to have the farmers carry our forty pound rucksacks up the hill for us. They smiled and complied, carrying three packs each. When we reached the top we were dripping in sweat with rubbery legs; while the two Vietnamese were hardly distressed by the arduous climb. We all reached into our pockets and generously paid them for their labor. I now can not help but wonder if they would have carried our burden if they were not intimidated by gun toting giants?

My time in Vietnam included more combat than most American troops, but not as much as many, and certainly nothing like Dien Bien Phu where all French force defenders were killed, wounded or captured. I always suppressed my fear of being taken prisoner but had heard rumors of the treatment of captured American pilots at the infamous Hanoi Prison, sardonically dubbed the "Hanoi Hilton". Dr. Fall brought home the reality of the fate of French Union Forces at the hands of the communists. Of the 37,000 French prisoners of war, 27,000 died in captivity. Paratroopers were particularly hated by the Viet-Minh. Dr. Fall best illustrates that at the Battle of To-Le in October, 1952 one hundred and ten paratroopers had been taken prisoner, only four survived to liberation in August, 1954. I'm sure captured Vietnamese members of the French Union Forces fared no better. Compassion, always short in supply while in war, seemed to be particularly lacking with the communist party political commissars, who were in charge of indoctrination of both their own troops and P.O.W.s. Dr. Fall refers to one battle lost by the French. A doctor, Major Varme-Janville stayed behind with immobile French wounded as the shattered remains of the unit retreated.

> "Vamre-Janville's sacrifice had been in vain. To be sure. The 803rd (Viet-Minh Battalion) did not kill the wounded on the spot; in fact, it used many trucks still in running condition to return the wounded to the empty hospital in Ankhe'. Varme-Janville begged the Communists to let him operate on his wounded, offering that he would operate and care for the Viet-Minh wounded as well.

> But at AnKhe' he no longer dealt with the frontline Viet-Minh but with the Communist Political Commissars. The answer was simple:

> 'You are no longer a doctor, but simply a dirty imperialist officer. Our wounded have no doctor. Your wounded have no doctor."

It seems strange that combat units of any army would travel with officers whose only concern was the political righteousness of its troops. What would happen if some worn out, bedraggled private, after dodging artillery fire, air assaults and climbing mountains all day and night called Uncle Ho or General Giap horses asses for making him do it? Would he be shot or jailed?

When you count all the times President Johnson; the Commander of all Vietnam Forces, General Westmoreland; and our Battalion Commander, Colonel Stiles names were taken in vain, there would be no one left to fight. Political Commissar is just a name for someone spying on his own people.

Somehow lecturing captured prisoners of war on the wonders of Communism, after being beaten, tortured and starved would fall of deaf ears and closed minds. It would be naive to believe that in some instance we, the United States, did not mistreat some of the Viet Cong prisoners. There is always an overzealous rogue thinking this is the quickest way to get information. The units in which I served captured a fair number of Viet Cong and no mistreatment occurred. The United States abides by the tenets of the Geneva Convention with regard to Prisoners of War. There was no institutional policy of torturous inter-rogation and if any one needs lectures on the virtues of Capitalism, I suspect it is many of our own college students.

By the summer of 1953, according to Dr. Fall, it was obvious to the French senior officers that - there was no hope of victory. As one commander explained it:

> "This is not a military war in the old sense. It is not even a political war. What we're facing here is a social war, a class war. As long as we don't destroy the Mandarin class, abolish excessive tenancy rates and do fail to give every farmer his plot of land, this country'll go communist as soon as we turn our backs.
>
> As long as we don't give the Vietnamese the only program they could really be expected to fight for, we're doomed to fight this war without any hopes for success and die here like merce-naries."

As I walked and patrolled the boondocks of the central highland of Vietnam, I never gave much thought to who owned the land. I assumed the rice paddies were tended by families of subsistence farmers. The land and animals, particularly the huge beast of burden, the water buffalo, were property of the farmer, not some communal enterprise. The domestic water buffalo are two thousand pound brutes with large thick horns that sweep back in an arc towards their powerful neck and shoulders. It always amazed me to watch village children ride or lead these docile animals around by the ring in their nose. The animals seemed more hostile when we Americans were around. Perhaps the scent of us primarily meat eaters was different than the fish and rice diet of the locals. My most alarming encounter with this beast came on a squad size patrol crossing a dry bedded rice field. Two hundred meters away a grazing herd of about twenty buffalo began stampeding in our direction. An Olympic sprinter could cover that distance in twenty seconds. We had no way of knowing how fast the buffalo were, and we were not Olympic sprinters. With no where to hide, we began firing in their direction. Undeterred, they continued the charge until two well placed shots from Spec 4 Conway's M-79 grenade launcher landed in front of them. The two quick explosions startled the buffalo and they veered off to the left of our position then slowing down came to a halt and began milling around as if all was normal. We, on the other hand made a rapid retreat to the nearest treeline, just in case our adversary decided to regroup. Like that French Commander who feared dying like a mercenary, I had no desire to die in a cattle stampede.

A senior tank commander with the very unFrench name of Colonel Wainwright ("My grandfather was an English officer captured by Napoleon who never got over his taste for French women and stayed after the whole thing was over.") expressed the French effort in Vietnam best:

> *"There is a difference between us French and Don Quixote. Don Quixote rode against windmills believing they were giants, but we ride against windmills knowing they are windmills but doing it all the same because we think that there ought to be someone in this materialistic world who rides against windmills."*

Time will tell if we, the American, fought giants or windmills. I had no aspiration to fight either. I just wanted to do what was expected and go home with body, mind and above all soul intact.

Like most veterans, I kept most of my thoughts about Vietnam to myself. Occasionally someone would ask what I thought about the war. I'm sure most were sincere in wanting to know, but I do believe some were really asking "What do you think of us who didn't serve?" While

I would hem and haw and mumble some inanity, my real thoughts turn to the words Shakespeare put into the mouth of Henry the V at the Battle of Agincourt in the 15th century. No one knows what King Henry actually said, but it must have been the best half time speech of all times. His exhausted, sick and starved troops, outnumbered ten to one, routed the French on their home court.

> *What's he that wishes so?*
> *My cousin Westmoreland? No, my fair cousin;*
> *If we are marked to die, we are now*
> *To do our country loss; and if to live,*
> *The fewer men, the greater share of honour.*
> *God's will! I pray thee, wish not one man more*
> *By Jove, I am not covetous for gold,*
> *Nor care I who doth feed upon my cost;*
> *It yearns me not if men my garments wear;*
> *Such outward things dwell not in my desires.*
> *But if it be a sin to cover honour,*
> *I am the most offending soul alive.*
> *No, faith, my coz, wish not a man from England.*
> *God's peace! I would not lose so great an honour*
> *As one man more methinks would share from me*
> *For the best hope I have. O, do not wish one more!*
> *Rather proclaim it, Westmoreland, through my host,*
> *That he which hath no stomach to this fight,*
> *Let him depart; his passport shall be made,*
> *And crowns for convoy put into his purse;*
> *We would not die in that man's company*
> *That fears his fellowship to die with us.*
> *This day is call'd the feast of Crispian.*
> *He that out lives this day, and comes safe home,*
> *Will stand a tip-toe when this is nam'd,*
> *And rouse him at the name of Crispian.*
> *He that shall live this day, and see old age,*
> *Will yearly on the vigil feast his neighbours,*
> *And say 'To-morrow is Saint Crispian'*
> *Then will he strip his sleeve and show his scars.*

And say 'Those wounds I had on Crispian's Day'
Old men forget; yet all shall be forgot,
But he'll remember, with advantages,
What feats he did that day. Then shall our names,
Familiar in his mouth as household words-
Harry the King, Bedford and Exeter,
Warwick and Talbot, Salisbury and Gloucester -
Be in their flowing cups freshly rememb'red.
This story shall the good men teach his son;
And Crispin Crispian shall ne'er go by,
From this day to the ending of the world,
But we in it shall be remembered -
We few, we happy few, we band of brothers;
For he to-day that sheds his blood with me
Shall be my brother, be he ne'er so vile,
This day shall gentle his condition;
And gentlemen in England now-a-bed
Shall think themselves accurs'd they were not here,
And hold their manhood cheap whiles any speaks
That fought with us upon Saint Crispin's Day.

I had no judgment or animosity toward those who chose different-ly. We all must live with our choices throughout life. In this matter, I am O.K. with mine. King Henry was fighting for land and privilege he perceived to be his. The United States laid no claim to any land or resource of Vietnam. From my point of view, flawed according to some, we were merely stopping the spread of a vile communist takeover of a free people. I am proud to be a part of it.

The defeat of the French at Dien Bien Phu came on May 8th, 1954. On July 20th, a cease fire was negotiated in Geneva. The French began to withdraw from Vietnam. Most of the actual fighting had been done north of the 17th parallel in what is now North Vietnam. A functional government was established in the southern half of Vietnam under the rule of Ngo Dinh Diem. According to their cease fire agreement, a general election was to be held in 1956 to unite all of Vietnam. Since neither the government of the Republic of South Vietnam, nor the United States had signed the agreement, the South refused to abide by the agreement and the specified election was not be held. The United States now had a clear cut, indigenous, anti-communist government to support. Act II of the Indochina War was about to commence.

The United States encouraged the French to fight on in Vietnam, but when U. S. air power could have saved the day at Dien Bien Phu, the United States abandoned their allies as Giap had guessed. The Viet-Minh positions in the mountains were vulnerable to air strikes. We could have helped. A defeat of the Viet-Minh at Dien Bien Phu might have brought about a more suitable conclusion to the first Indochina War. But who can tell?

The lack of air support by the United States at Dien Bien Phu was an example of General DeGaulle's observation regarding American politicians and Presidents: "In a crisis not involving her directly, the United States cannot be counted on with full certainty."

All fledgling nations need varying degrees of support. It is questionable whether Americans would have gained their independence without the financial and military support of the French. The role played by General Baron von Steuben, though not a General nor Baron, was certainly significant. He transformed Washington's beleaguered and undisciplined army at Valley Forge. In less than one year these troops became a military machine that understood and executed European battle drills well enough to stand toe to toe with the most powerful army in the world. Washington's troops proved their mettle on the fields of Monmouth, New Jersey the following summer.

There were other Europeans who came to help such as the Polish nobleman Casimir Pulaski. Pulaski was quickly promoted to a Brigadier General in the Continental Army after his daring cavalry charge saved the retreating Americans at the Battle of Brandywine. Pulaski became known as "The Father of the American Cavalry". Thaddeus Koscinzko, another nobleman from Poland who came to the aid of the American rebels, had been educated at the newly instituted Corps of Cadets in Warsaw as a military officer. He continued his education in Paris and eventually found his way to America and the Continental Army in 1776 as an engineer. He was appointed Head Engineer in the Army. Among other contributions, he designed the defenses of Saratoga and at West Point. One could argue these men and others like them were mere adventurers, soldiers of fortune, mercenaries. The fact remains that they fought and some died, including Pulaski, in defense of the freedom of others. That makes them heroes.

Americans returned the favor many times over in World War I and World War II. We support Israeli independence in the face of overtly hostile Muslim nations who outnumber the six million Israelis by about 200,000,000 on a sliver of land the size of New Jersey. Yet after the wars in the Middle East of 1948, 1956, 1967 and 1973 the United States did not have to commit ground troops. Financial aid, equipment and I'm sure intelligence, is all they required.

After four years of war with North Korea and China, Americans and members of other countries in the United Nations preserved the liberty of South Korea. The South Koreans had to fight for themselves. While a small contingent of U. S. troops remain at the Demilitarized Zone, the 38th parallel divides North and South Korea. The defense of the peninsula is largely a South Korean responsibility. In fact, South Korea is so stable, it was able to provide approximately 50,000 troops to Vietnam during peak deployment.

Should not our future allegiances be based on the willingness of our allies to defend themselves. While in Vietnam, my contact with the Vietnamese soldiers was limited at best. I was influenced by Max's skepticism of the fighting ability of the AVRN troops. Rumors floated among us about their lack of willingness to engage the NVA. In the Spring of 1972, most American troops, especially ground combat troops had been withdrawn by President Nixon. The North saw this as an opportunity to launch a massive strike against the South. The ARVN proved their worth with the United States' air and naval support. The ARVN inflicted nearly 100,000 casualties on the NVA. The Army of the Republic of Viet Nam held their ground and resoundingly defeated the Communists. Good reason to believe that as long as the U. S. is willing to blunt the material support of Russia and China to North Vietnam, South Vietnam would remain free despite its real or perceived short comings. Candid and reflective Max once stated, "If you won't fight for yourself why would I fight for you?"

Mao Tse-tung declared "Political power comes from the barrel of a gun." Most of history's dictators and those currently in power; Castro, Ho Chi Minh, Kim Jung Il of North Korea and the communist party in general subscribe to that philosophy. Guns can be a means of intimidation and subjugation. Nations can not be successful societies if your border guards are training their weapons on people trying to escape their domination rather than keeping undesirables out. One million North Vietnamese fled to the south after the defeat of the French. Tens of thousands risked all in flimsy boats leaving Castro's Cuba. The same occurred all over communist controlled Eastern Europe most recently after the Hungarian revolt in 1956 and the Czechoslovakian uprising in 1968.

I believe we have a covenant with God to help these people become secure in freedom. A legacy, like it or not, passed on to us by those who insured liberty to the United States. After all, the French were not mere cheerleaders during our revolution. During the final battle in Yorktown the French navy and infantry actually outnumbered the Americans three to one. The French Commander Count Jean-Baptiste Donatien DeVimeurde DeRochambeau designed the strategy that led to victory over the British camped there.

In many ways the French alliance seemed odd. The American colonialists aided the British in the defeat of the French in North America during the French and Indian War twenty years before the American revolt. France was ruled by an Absolute Monarch, not the Republic envisioned by the colonists. France was a Catholic nation and the colonies were Protestant. The French had no thoughts of regaining the lost North American Territories. However, a defeat of Britain in America would blunt the expanding influence of their super power rival.

In 1917 when the American expeditionary force landed on French soil during World War I, the commander of the A.E.F., General John Pershing is quoted, "Nous voila, Lafayette!" (Lafayette, we are here!). I think the good general missed an opportunity by not saluting Rochambeau as well.

Admittedly these ponderous thoughts did not pervade my consciousness in Vietnam. The adventuresomeness of it all was overwhelming. But deep down in my soul and the soul of most combat troops a sense of duty and honor was instilled through our upbringing, our parents, the World War II generation, through our education, all the symbols and stories of our heritage and in our military training.

The question remains, when to let go? After the victory at Yorktown, the French did not stay and try to create a society in their own image. The French forces left satisfied that they gained a new trading partner, had exacted a measure of revenge on an adversary and could now compete with Britain on an equal footing.

❖   ❖   ❖

To fight in defense of our country. Why are you so afraid of
war and hostility?

HEKTOR, *THE ILIAD*

❖   ❖   ❖

Some professors did seem to give us veterans a little leeway in class when possible. So clearly, there was no animus toward us. I am sure there were anti-war rallies around campus, but none stand out. Then again, this was conservative Kentucky and not the hot bed of protests that marked Cal-Berkeley or Columbia.

I have heard a lot of talk regarding how returning Vietnam Vets were treated; being called baby killers, being spat upon, and worse. I have no personal experience with any of that. The taunts of "baby killer" are particularly heinous when I think about Sergeant Morgan and how he lost his life in that alien village. His cautious approach to avoid civilian casualties cost him and us dearly. I'm glad no one had the nerve to confront me with that slur. They would not have liked the response.

Unfortunately, there is no denying the massacre in the tiny hamlet of My Lai where Charlie Company of the 11th Brigade from the Army's American Division killed, raped and tortured up to five hundred civilian women, children and old men. A helicopter pilot, Hugh Thompson, stopped the rampage by positioning his aircraft between the advancing troops and the fleeing civilians and ordering his door gunner to fire on any troops that continued to pursue the villagers.

In late 1969 Thompson gave testimony before the United States House of Representatives Armed Services Committee. He summed up the thoughts and feelings of most Vets at Western in his last paragraph to the committee;

"It was probably one of the saddest days of my life. I just could not believe that people could totally lose control and I've heard people say this happened all the time. I don't believe it. I'm not naive to understand that innocent civilians did not get killed in Vietnam. I truly pray to God that My Lai was not an every day occurrence. I don't know if any could keep their sanity if something like that happens all the time. I can see where four or five people get killed, something like that. But that was nothing like that, it was no accident whatso-ever. Pure premeditated murder. And we're trained better

than that and it's just not something you'd like to do"

Around this time I was vaguely aware of John Kerry, an ex-navy guy who was a member of a group called Vietnam Veterans Against the War. They are said to have thrown their medals on the lawn of the White House and compared our troops, I guess that includes me, to the hordes of Genghis Khan – killing indiscriminately, burning and looting helpless villagers.

The country, still reeling from the shocking revelations of My Lai now faced another stunning incident closer to home at Kent State University in Ohio. On May 3rd, 1970 an arsonist set fire to the ROTC building on campus, supposedly in protest to President Nixon's decision to send troops across the Cambodian border to attack the North Vietnamese in their sanctuary. To me a logical military decision. As Sun Tze said of the enemy, "If he is taking his ease, give him no rest." "Attack him where he is unprepared, appear where you are not expected." To some students at Kent State it was an expansion of the war. Approximately 1,000 students surrounded the building and cheered as it burned down. They also stoned the police and firemen attempting to extinguish the fire. The Governor called on the National Guard to restore order. Unfortunately the poorly trained and inexperienced guardsmen, confronted with a large crowd of students panicked and fired on the protesters killing four and wounding nine on May 4, 1970. Max's words would reverberate in my brain again, "Stay out of the villages. Hostile civilians and combat troops don't mix well."

The shootings set off student protests nationwide. On May 8th, eleven student protesters were bayoneted on the campus of the University of New Mexico by the New Mexico National Guard. At Jackson State University in Jackson, Mississippi two students were killed and twelve wounded by the police. On May 9th 100,000 people demonstrated in Washington, D.C. The protest more accurately resembled a riot as demonstrators burned cars and smashed windows. Charles Colson, Counsel to President Nixon stated;

"The 82nd Airborne was in the basement of the Executive Office Building, so I went down just to talk to some of the guys and walk among them, and they're lying on the floor leaning on their packs and their helmets and their cartridge

belts and their rifles cocked and you're thinking, this can't be the United States of America. This is not the greatest free democracy in the world. This is a nation at war with itself."

I find it interesting that my brothers in the 82ⁿᵈ Airborne are always called upon when troubles arise. Business and classes continued without interruption at Western, unlike 900 other universities which closed down for a day or more.

Western's campus was not completely protest free. One day some 200 student demonstrators gathered in front of the Administration Building to hear several outside speakers. Another group of protesters marched to the ROTC offices and cajoled the cadets to join the demonstrators. One sentiment expressed on a sign in front of the offices;

WARS WILL CEASE WHEN MEN REFUSE TO FIGHT

I'm all for it, now if only the bad guys would buy in. Unlike Kent State and some other universities no buildings were burned, rocks thrown, nor was there need for the Kentucky National Guardsmen to be called to restore order.

A Gallop Poll taken shortly after the Kent State incident showed that 58% of citizens blamed the students, 31% blamed the Ohio National Guard, and 11% had no opinion. I am sure Max would agree with my view, if you engage in provocative behavior such as burning a building and cars, smashing windows and throwing rocks, you are going to get a reaction. To feign outrage is disingenuous. When you light a fire, you will get a flame.

"Duty, honor, country.
Those three hallowed words,
reverently dictate what you ought to be,
what you can be, what you will be."

General Douglas MacArthur in a speech to the cadets at West Point in 1962.

The officers and troops of Charlie Company, 11ᵗʰ Brigade did not do their duty and they dishonored their country. There is no rational excuse for their unwarranted savagery. They broke the code of honor and chivalry and should be punished accordingly.

It was hard to differentiate the motivations for the antiwar groups. True pacifism – refusing to fight under any circumstance. Opposition to this particular war. Those who stayed in the country and faced the consequences of their objection. Those who fled to Canada to avoid the draft. I'm sure some people actually believed the U. S. was making war on the Vietnamese people and did not distinguish between the invading northern communists and the people of the south. I'm not sure why they would not make the distinction, but discerning the true nature of the war by listening to the news media was not always easy then nor is it to this day.

There seemed to be a notion that if we just tried to understand each other better as people, we could all sit down as nations and peacefully negotiate our problems. I don't think Alexander, Caesar, Napoleon and Hitler were misunderstood or harbored any intention to negotiate. Wars are fought because there is something in the psyche, some innate human desire for power and control over others. These people are all around us in our cities, towns, neighborhoods and families. Under the right circumstances the more cunning and persuasive rise in power to become tyrants both petty and grand.

Tyrants need enablers, propagandists, and as Lenin supposedly called them "useful idiots" - a term applied to naive and gullible people who believed the utopian lies of the Marxists. The North Vietnamese found such a prized individual in the American actress Jane Fonda, daughter of screen legend Henry Fonda. Some 1970's news photos showed the actress Jane Fonda sitting on a NVA antiaircraft gun battery in Hanoi. She was not actually firing at anyone, but to me she looked pretty silly sitting there wearing a gunners' helmet. Meanwhile the battery crew leered at her as if she were an exotic dancer in costume. Sedition? Treason? Pacifist heroine? We all can make our own judgments, but Lenin's view seems an apt description.

Jerry Rubin, Abby Hoffman and others of their activist brand called "Revolution for the hell of it!" There are many others, perhaps not so naive and gullible but more sinister in motives. Groups such as the Weather Underground or Weathermen led by Bill Ayers, Bernadette

Dorne and Jeff Jones, among others, were responsible for bombings, violence and death. An interesting way to promote antiwar and peaceful sentiments, or did they have something else in mind? The war was the excuse needed to transform the United States from a Constitutional Republic into a more progressive society where the educated elite, such as themselves, make the decisions. They viewed most citizens as not knowing their own best interest. Most citizens must be prodded or forced to do the right thing. They believed a strong bureaucracy is needed to control the behavior of others.

In my mind, they think of themselves as the eternal Olympian Gods of Ancient Greece who control the fate of their mere mortal subjects. The gods had all the same virtues and vices of humans but suffered no ill effects of their actions, decisions and manipulations. The Greeks bore the consequences for the gods' capriciousness. Many leaders of the peace movement were dazzled by their own brilliance. They felt that if they thought it, it must be right. No introspection necessary. While we humble humans struggle with our conscience. Admiration for Mao, Che and Castro three of the 20th century's most prolific mass murderers, rivaled only by Stalin and Hitler, is hard to defend. To replace the legacy of Washington, Franklin, Jefferson and Madison with the troubled doctrine and practices of Lenin and Mao is absurd.

The Utopian principle, "From each according to his ability, to each according to his needs", popularized by Karl Marx suggests a pirate mentality. There are limited resources to go around, therefore one must take from one group to give to another. No credit is given to a free people pursuing their own goals and ambitions could actually produce an abundance from which all benefit. The Marxist view is that for someone to gain, someone else must relinquish. This Socialist principle led to the collectivism of all lands and means of production in the Soviet Union, Cuba, China, Eastern Europe and now North Vietnam. The State becomes arbiter of who gets what. Government "experts" and bureaucrats are appointed to administer programs... gee not much chance of anything going wrong there.

Jefferson, Madison and the other framers of the Constitution recognized that a small central government was the necessary course to allow liberty for people to determine, according to their own ability and ambition, what their needs were. The language in the preamble to the

Constitution is precise, "Provide for the common defense, promote the general welfare" not provide the general welfare. The founders knew the environment between Massachusetts and Virginia was unique and needed to be administered from a local perspective. A central planned government needs to govern from conformity.

My Oath of Induction resurfaced in my memory. American troops swore allegiance to the United States Constitution compared to the German soldiers of 1934 who swore fidelity to one man, Adolph Hitler. I wondered to whom the Weather Underground would have us take a sacred oath?

The peace at any price movement has many and deep roots. The deepest connection can be found during the Civil War or the "War of Northern Aggression" as my Kentucky friends, with tongue planted firmly in cheek refer to it. Many northerners opposed the war and were clearly in favor of allowing the Confederacy to keep slavery if that was what it would take to end hostilities. They were named the Copperheads for the poisonous snake that strikes without warning. They were mostly Democrats who opposed President Lincoln. They tried to damage the war effort. They encouraged men to dodge the draft and encouraged desertion among the men already in uniform. Their influence was strong at first. Many northern newspapers and politicians rallied to the cause. After the southern defeat at Gettysburg, and Sherman's march to the sea in Georgia, the strength of the Copperheads waned. This is in curious contrast to Vietnam where the peace movement gained momentum after victories by U. S. forces at TET.

Oddly, the Democrats nominated General George McClellan to run against President Lincoln in the election of 1864. The platform of the Democrats consisted mostly of the Copperhead agenda. McClellan was pro-war and for the restoration of the Union, but not for the abolition of slavery. The President had fired McClellan from his position of Commander of the Army of the Potomac for insubordination and, as Lincoln perceived it, a lack of willingness to fight. The President once remarked, "If General McClellan does not want to use the Army, I would like to borrow it for a time." For the General's part in this conflict, he often referred to Lincoln as, "Nothing more than a well meaning baboon." Not the makings of a harmonious working relationship.

Almost 100 years later the Democrats were again in disarray. Despite the two Democratic administrations of John Kennedy and Lyndon Johnson, whose policies led to American involvement in Vietnam, it was the Democrats who largely wanted the United States to disengage in Vietnam. Hubert Humphrey became the Presidential nominee for the Democrats, the Vice President under Johnson who supported all of Johnson's policies. I am not sure what he wanted to do with regard to the war in Vietnam. The politics of war are often very perplexing. As in the Civil War, the more united Republican Party carried the day and Nixon won the election of 1968. I suppose there have always been those who believe that peace is merely the absence of war. Peace, at least to me, also means freedom from the absolute control of others. The attitude of the peace movement, even after one hundred years, remains the same. The clothes, the hair styles, the droopy mustaches change but not the self righteous posture. Then again, as I look around campus and note the attire of many students, maybe nothing has changed.

The fall semester of 1972 saw some changes both personal and with the war. Friends from one of the fraternities asked if I would be interested in a job as their Resident Advisor. The university was appointing graduate students as R.A.s in the ten fraternities. The position came with a suite of rooms, tuition, book expenses and $150.00/month. I was not a graduate student, but the fraternity members hoped my advanced age of twenty six would persuade the Administrator of Greek Affairs. It did. That the Administrator was also a veteran might have helped.

The fraternity was not an "Animal House". The members had good GPAs and they were competitive in all endeavors. I even coached their intramural football team. The title Resident Advisor seemed a little cumbersome so the boys began calling me Dad. Walking across campus and having someone shout out, "Hey, Dad!" was a little startling at first and certainly drew a curious stare or two from the uninitiated. It always brought a smile to my face. Ray and Big A had jobs. Ray as a night shift manager at a local trucking company and Big A with me at the Hilltopper Pub. They both decided they could afford their own apartments.

In November 1972, the North Vietnamese left the negotiating table. President Nixon ordered mass bombing raids on military targets in Hanoi and Haiphong over Christmas week to demonstrate his resolve to bring the communists back to the table. His strategy worked, the North Vietnamese came back and met with Nixon's envoy, Henry Kissinger. On January 13, 1974 an agreement to end hostilities was reached. The South Vietnamese leaders seemed reluctant to agree to some of the fine points of the accord, particularly that the North Vietnamese could leave troops in the south. Why that provision was in place was a puzzle to all who knew about it. Eventually, with assurance from Nixon that the United States would aid them if the North violated the treaty, the South Vietnamese delegation gave in. Perhaps President Nguyen Van Thieu was not aware of DeGaulle's assessment of the United States' political will.

CHAPTER VIII

Max, Kennedy and DeGaulle Were Right

The Airborne behemoth descended on the runway of Clark Air Force Base in the Philippines. The massive Air Force C141 four engine jet transport that I and many others parachuted from carried not the apprehensive troopers waiting their turn in the door, but anxious passengers of a different sort. The date was February 12, 1973 and the first Prisoners of War from the notorious Hanoi Hilton were on the first leg of their odyssey home. Ray and I met several other vets at Big A's apartment and sipped our beers in silence as the first few POWs were carried off in stretchers, then a parade of men; some limping, some walking stiffly, but most seemed to be in decent shape. Slim, but not skeletal as I had anticipated. I still feared and wondered how many of those captured would return home, hoping they had not experienced the same fate as the French POWs suffered two decades before.

I thought of my own homecomings, the first as a solitary soldier in a Class "A" uniform, the second as a walking wounded in hospital PJs and robe. I was thankful I was not among these courageous souls – mostly Navy and Air Force pilots, in gray windbreakers and dark blue pants. Many had spent five to eight years in captivity. Later that night the first POWs returning from imprisonment by the South Vietnamese Viet Cong came to Clark. I suspected they were predominantly enlisted men captured on the ground as opposed to the pilots shot out of the sky. They appeared gaunt and frail in their olive drab green pajama style clothing. In the months that followed both groups had horrific tales of torture, deprivation and starvation to tell.

The general consensus among my friends was that Nixon had done his job. He extricated the United States from Vietnam with honor. He kept the north guessing. His visit to Communist China was a brilliant move. The North Vietnamese did not know what to make of it. Were Washington and Bejing, Vietnam's ancient nemesis, making a secret agreement with regard to Vietnam? I am sure Moscow was also a little upset. So much for communist solidarity. Nixon accomplished all of this while withdrawing United States ground combat troops and turning the war over to the AVRN forces.

In August 1973, the veto-proof Democratic congress passed the Case-Church amendment, prohibiting any further military involvement in Southeast Asia. This amendment undermined the basic underlying principle of the peace accords. This did not bode well for the South. Leaders of both the South and North understood that peace treaties and truces just allowed time for the losing side to rest, recuperate and gather strength to strike another blow. The defeat and unconditional surrender of a pertinacious aggressor is the surest answer to a lasting peace.

Memories of Vietnam started to fade five years after my last tour. The images of rice paddies, helicopters, troops in green jungle fatigues flashing across the T. V. screen would no longer be a nightly feature. Only an occasional nocturnal stirring, not exactly a nightmare, would cause me to bolt upright in bed. My dreams of Vietnam carried three main themes; I would walk through the mayhem of a fire fight in plain view but go unnoticed or ignored by "Charlie". Often my weapon would misfire and a sense of anxiety would briefly fill my thoughts when I awoke; other times I would find myself in the jungle fighting hand to hand with several V.C. No one was ever injured. They would jump on me and I would be able to throw them off like rag dolls. They are not able to overcome me but I am unable to knock them out. My waking moments were that of frustration; the more pleasant and peaceful nightly fantasy had me floating through billowy cumulus clouds. While not exactly flying, I could bound high in to the sky and pull myself through the air for great distances by means of a combination of the breast and butterfly swimming strokes. When I eventually hit the ground I could jump once more and soar over the Vietnam landscape – jungle, villages and all. For this illusion I fought to remain asleep.

Vietnam was not quite through with me. Dave Gibbons, a freshman and Vietnam vet who served with the 101st Airborne Division stopped in the Pub while I was tending bar. It was a quiet Tuesday evening. With few customers to wait on Dave and I had a chance to talk. A Kentucky native, Dave finished his army commitment at nearby Fort Campbell and decided Western was the right fit for him to take advantage of the G. I. Bill. We exchanged the usual "what unit?", and "what year were you in Vietnam?" When Dave learned I had served with the Airborne Brigade of the 1st Cavalry he mentioned that a platoon Sergeant in his Company had been reassigned from the first Cav, a lifer who had been in Vietnam since 1965, Sergeant Maxwell.

If it is true that everyone on this earth knows everyone else by six degrees of separation, then the world of paratroopers is separated by a factor of one. The mere mention of Max's name brought up a flood of memories and our connection through Max gave me the permission to unleash stories long held back. I told him about one night when my squad and Palmer's were led by Max to set up an ambush on a hillside. My squad remained with Max while Palmer's moved into the valley to form an "L" shaped trap where we could fire on any ambushees from front and side. Our positions were predetermined on the map earlier in the day. After much whispering with Palmer over the radio, it seemed Palmer was not exactly where Max wanted. Seemingly frustrated, Max bellowed out across the valley, "Palmer, get your head out of your ass and move fifty meters to the left!" The RTO and I stared at Max in total astonishment. Had all these years and tours of combat finally pushed him over the brink of sanity? Though the twilight was fading to darkness, Max could sense our bewilderment and said, "Hell, I guess if Charlie is moving through the valley, he'll probably go another route. There is nothing left for us to do but get a good nights rest... two men on in two hour shifts." Sometimes one can fulfill the letter of a mission and avoid the difficult reality of it. We were sent out to set up an ambush. No one said we actually had to ambush anyone. Another rule of survival: avoid conflict.

I related to Dave how Max preached to us not to underestimate those "little sons of bitches". But don't exaggerate their abilities either. That was a little perplexing to me at first. One day, after an unusual entire company size patrol, we camped just outside on the east side of a small village. At twilight, just when we were all settled in for the night, the order came to pack up and move. Some of us began to grumble. Max quickly snapped a withering glance that let us know to shut up and move. Darkness now fell, only a few lights from the village shone on this moonless night. At first we moved a couple hundred meters further east and then north for about 100 meters more. Within the hour of our maneuver, AK-47 shots began pouring into our former encampment. We now had them outflanked and began a withering barrage of our own. Charlie obviously startled, began a weak response to our new location, but no longer had the stomach for the fight and fled west. We did not pursue. The only thing visible at this point would be the flash of a rifle muzzle. The next morning I saw Max grinning at us. He did not have to say a word. If Charlie could not hear or see 120 men stumbling through the darkness, then he was no better than us at night – no x-ray vision or innate ability that we did not possess. As a child I feared the dark and the boogie man that lurked there. The boogie man still exists in the shadows of Vietnam but we are just as tough and resourceful and better armed. Another lesson learned, another rule of survival implemented: use the murkiness of the night to take the offensive, not fear it.

I could now sense Dave's impatience, but I was on a roll. He would have plenty of time to tell his story. I was just about to tell the fable of the Buddhist Monks when Dave, who could no longer rein in his irritation, interrupted me, "Matt, you are not going to like this. The details are a little bit muddled, but the gist of the matter is that Maxwell was accused of murdering two Vietnamese civilians, a man and his teenage son, while leading a patrol in a supposedly hostile village. Word filtered down that he was court marshaled in Saigon, found guilty, and sent back to the states. What happened to him after that, I don't know. The guys on patrol with him were all sent to Saigon to testify or be charged as accessories. They never returned to the Company. I'm sure the company officers and NCOs knew what happened, but no one was talking. One rumor had Maxwell executing them because he was pissed they weren't giving up information. Another rumor said one of the rookies on the patrol had a nervous trigger finger, shot them, and Maxwell tried to cover it up. Anyway, this happened over two years ago. I don't think we will ever know the whole story." A hot flash followed by a clammy sensation enveloped me. It was the same feeling I have had many times before when invaded by thoughts of the events of the night Sergeant Morgan was killed. I have often wished I had shot at the silhouette crossing my path. How would that have changed the circumstances? The answer always comes back the same. I did as my conscience dictated. Firing at a possible innocent target was something I could not do. We must act only as our soul will allow. The result, the destiny is in God's province. This is a burden all warriors must carry. If you fail to follow your conscience and do not ask for forgiveness from the Almighty, your spirit will be doomed to torment. There is no reason to believe that Max did nothing less than follow the dictates of his conscience.

Without question there is great value in a college education. The four years, or in my case six, pursuing a degree aid in the maturation of an individual. However, I contend that the military speeds up that process. Broken down, the army trains an individual in about six months for any particular job. After that, some recruits serve a six to eight month apprenticeship for leadership roles. Second Lieutenants and the apprentices of the Officer Corps, guided by the Company Commander and the Platoon Sergeant. After four years of college, I am not sure what sense of responsibility or leadership skills one acquires. Those attributes are gained very quickly in infantry units. The army turns boys to men and men to leaders. I don't think universities can make the same claim. When you consider that combat duty is slightly more hazardous than accounting, it is a remarkably fast process. I am grateful to have experienced both worlds, academia and the airborne. Though if I had to choose one to the exclusion of the other and leave my sanity open for question, I liked being a "Devil in Baggy Pants" too much to give it up.

My college career was coming to an end December, 1974. Reporting on Vietnam was limited. Still it came as no shock to me that North Vietnam broke the Paris Peace Accords and invaded South Vietnam. Probably to test the resolve of the United States. At first the ARVN troops fought well, but soon they were overwhelmed by the communists who had massive resupplies from their Russian allies. The Democratic controlled congress reneged on our promise to aid the South Vietnamese if the treaty were broken. Unfortunately, Nixon had resigned under the duress of the Watergate Scandal and the new President, Gerald Ford, did not have the power to force congress to act in accordance with the treaty. Just as at Dien Bien Phu during the first Indochina War, American air power could have made a difference. The emboldened North, seeing no interference from the United States, attacked the poorly equipped ARVN troops in open columns. It seems the Democratic-controlled congress had forgotten the words of then Senator John F. Kennedy at the Conference on Vietnam held in the Hotel Willard, Washington, D. C., June 1, 1956:

> *It is a genuine pleasure to be here today at this vital Conference on the future of Vietnam, and America's stake in that new nation, sponsored by the American Friends of Vietnam, an organization of which I am proud to be a member. Your meeting today at a time when political events concerning Vietnam are approaching a climax, both in that country and in our own Congress, is most timely. Your topic and deliberations, which emphasize the promise of the future more than the failures of the past, are most constructive. I can assure you that the Congress of the United States will give considerable weight to your findings and recommendations; and I extend to all of you who have made the effort to participate in this Conference my congratulations and best wishes.*

> *It is an ironic and tragic fact that this Conference is being held at a time when the news about Vietnam has virtually disappeared from the front pages of the American press, and the American people have all but forgotten the tiny nation for which we are in large measure responsible. This decline in public attention is due, I believe, to three factors:*

First, it is due in part to the amazing success of President Diem in meeting firmly and with determination the major political and economic crises which had heretofore continually plagued Vietnam. (I shall say more about this point later, for it deserves more consideration from all Americans interested in the future of Asia.)

Second, it is due in part to the traditional role of American journalism, including readers as well as writers, to be more interested in crises than in accomplishments, to give more space to the threat of wars than the need for works, and to larger headlines on the sensational omissions of the past than the creative missions of the future.

Third and finally, our neglect of Vietnam is the result of one of the most serious weaknesses that has hampered the long-range effectiveness of American foreign policy over the past several years – and that is the over emphasis upon our role as "volunteer fire department" for the world. Whenever and wherever fire breaks out – in Indo-China, in the Middle East, in Guatemala, in Cyprus, in the Formosan Straits – our firemen rush in, wheeling up all their heavy equipment, and resorting to every known method of containing and extinguishing the blaze. The crowd gathers – the usually successful efforts of our able volunteers are heartily applauded – and then the firemen rush off to the next conflagration, leaving the grateful but still stunned inhabitants to clean up the rubble, pick up the pieces and rebuild their homes with whatever resources are available.

The role, to be sure, is a necessary one; but it is not the only role to be played, and the others, cannot be ignored. A volunteer fire department halts, but rarely prevents fires. It repels but rarely rebuilds; it meets the problems of the present but not of the future. And while we are devoting our attention to the Communist arson in Korea, there is smoldering in Indo-China; we turn our efforts to Indo-China until the alarm sounds in Algeria – and so it goes.

Of course Vietnam is not completely forgotten by our policy-makers today — I could not in honesty make such a charge and the facts would easily refute it — but the unfortunate truth of the matter is that, in my opinion, Vietnam would in all likelihood be receiving more attention from our Congress and Administration, and greater assistance under our aid programs, if it were in imminent danger of Communist invasion or revolution. Like those peoples of Latin America and Africa whom we have very nearly overlooked in the past decade, the Vietnamese may find that their devotion to the cause of democracy, and their success in reducing the strength of local Communist groups, have had the ironic effect of reducing American support. Yet the need for that support has in no way been reduced. (I hope it will not be necessary for the Diem Government — or this organization — to subsidize the growth of the South Vietnamese Communist Party in order to focus American attention on that nation's critical needs!)

No one contends that we should now rush all our firefighting equipment to Vietnam, ignoring the Middle East or any other part of the world. But neither should we conclude that the cessation of hostilities in Indo-China removed that area from the list of important areas of United States foreign policy. Let us briefly consider exactly what is "America's Stake in Vietnam".

First, Vietnam represents the cornerstone of the Free World in Southeast Asia, the keystone to the arch, the finger in the dike. Burma, Thailand, India, Japan, the Philippines and obviously Laos and Cambodia are among those whose security would be threatened if the Red Tide of Communism overflowed into Vietnam. In the past, our policy-makers have sometimes issued contradictory statements on this point — but the long history of Chinese invasions of Southeast Asia being stopped by Vietnamese warriors should have removed all doubt on this subject.

Moreover, the independence of a Free Vietnam is crucial to the Free world in fields other than the military. Her economy is essential to the economy of Southeast Asia; and her political liberty is an inspiration to those seeking to obtain or maintain their liberty in all parts of Asia – and indeed the world. The fundamental tenets of this nations foreign policy, in short, depend in considerable measure upon a strong and free Vietnamese nation.

Secondly, Vietnam represents a proving ground of democracy in Asia. However we may choose to ignore it or deprecate it, the rising prestige and influence of Communist China in Asia are unchallengeable facts. Vietnam represents the alternative to Communist dictatorship. If this democratic experiment fails, if some one million refugees have fled the totalitarianism of the North only to find neither freedom nor security in the South, then weakness, not strength, will characterize the meaning of democracy in the minds of still more Asians. The United States is directly responsible for this experiment – it is playing an important role in the laboratory where it is being conducted. We cannot afford to permit the experiment to fail.

Third and in somewhat similar fashion, Vietnam represents a test of American responsibility and determination in Asia. If we are not the parents of little Vietnam, than surely we are the godparents, We presided at its birth, we gave assistance to its life, we have helped to shape its future, As French influence in the political, economic and military spheres has declined in Vietnam, American influence has steadily grown. This is our offspring – we cannot abandon it, we cannot ignore its needs. And if it falls victim to any perils that threaten its existence – Communism, political anarchy, poverty and the rest – then the United States, with some justification, will be held responsible, and our prestige in Asia will sink to a new low.

Fourth and finally, America's stake in Vietnam, in her strength and in her security, is a very selfish one – for it can be measured, in the last analysis, in terms of American lives and American dollars, it is now well known that we were at one time on the brink of war in Indo-China – a war which could well have been more costly, more exhausting and less conclusive than any war we have ever known. The threat to such war is not now altogether removed from the horizon. Military weakness, political instability or economic failure in the new state of Vietnam could change almost overnight the apparent security which has increasingly characterized that area under the leadership of Premier Diem. And the key position of Vietnam in Southeast Asia, as already discussed, makes inevitable the involvement of this nation's security in any new outbreak of trouble.

It is these four points, in my opinion, that represent America's stake in Vietnamese security. And before we look to the future, let us stop to review what the Diem Government has already accomplished by way of increasing that security. Most striking of all, perhaps, has been the rehabilitation of more than ¾ of a million refugees from the North. For these courageous people dedicated to the free way of life, approximately 45,000 houses have been constructed, 2,500 wells dug, 100 schools established and dozens of medical centers and maternity homes provided.

Equally impressive has been the increased solidarity of the Government, the elimination of rebellious sects and the taking of the first vital steps toward true democracy. Where once colonialism and Communism struggled for supremacy, a free and independent republic has been proclaimed, recognized by over 40 countries of the free world. Where once a playboy emperor ruled from a distant shore a constituent assembly has been elected.

Social and economic reforms have likewise been remarkable. The living conditions of the peasants have been vastly improved, the wastelands have been cultivated, and a wider ownership of the land is gradually being encouraged. Farm cooperatives and farmer loans have modernized an outmoded agricultural economy, and a tremendous dam in the center of the country has made possible the irrigation of a vast area previously uncultivated. Legislation for better labor relations, health protection, working conditions and wages has been completed under the leadership of President Diem.

Finally, the Vietnamese army – now fighting for its own homeland and not its colonial masters – has increased tremendously in both quality and quantity. General O'Daniel can tell you more about these accomplishments.

But the responsibility of the United States for Vietnam does not conclude, obviously, with a review of what has been accomplished thus far with our help. Much more needs to be done; much more in fact, than we have been doing up to now. Military alliances in Southeast Asia are necessary, but not enough. Atomic superiority and the development of new ultimate weapons are not enough. Informational and propaganda activities, warning of the evils of Communism and the blessings of the American way of life, are not enough in a country where concepts of free enterprise and capitalism are meaningless, where poverty and hunger are not enemies across the 17th parallel but enemies within their midst. As Ambassador Chuong has recently said: "People cannot be expected to fight for the Free World unless they have their own freedom to defend, their freedom from foreign domination as well as freedom from misery, oppression, corruption."

I shall not attempt to set forth the details of the type of aid program this nation should offer the Vietnamese – for it is not the details of that program that are as important as the spirit with which it is offered and the objectives it seeks to accomplish. We should not attempt to buy the friendship of the Vietnamese. Nor can we win their hearts by making them dependent upon our handouts. What we must offer them is a revolution – a political, economic and social revolution far superior to anything the Communists can offer – far more peaceful, far more democratic and far more locally controlled. Such a revolution will require much from the United States and much from Vietnam. We must supply capital to replace that drained by the centuries of colonial exploitation, technicians to train those handicapped by deliberate policies of illiteracy; guidance to assist a nation taking those first feeble steps toward the complexities of a republican form of government. We must assist the inspiring growth of Vietnamese democracy and economy, including the complete integration of those refugees who gave up their homes and their belongings to seek freedom. We must provide military assistance to rebuild the new Vietnamese Army, which every day faces the growing peril of Vietminh Armies across the border.

And finally, in the councils of the world, we must never permit any diplomatic action adverse to this, one of the youngest members of the family of nations – and I include in that injunction a plea that the United States never give its approval to the early nationwide elections called for by the Geneva Agreement of 1954. Neither the United States nor Free Vietnam was a party to that agreement – and neither the United States nor Free Vietnam is ever going to be a party to an election obviously stacked and subverted in advance, urged upon us by those who have already broken their own pledges under the Agreement they now seek to enforce.

All this and more we can offer Free Vietnam, as it passes through the present period of transition on its way to a new era – an era of pride and independence, an era of democratic and economic growth – an era which, when contrasted with the long years of colonial oppression, will truly represent a political, social and economic revolution.

This is the revolution we can, we should, we must offer to the people of Vietnam – not as charity, not as a business proposition, not as a political maneuver, nor simply to enlist them as soldiers against Communism of as chattels of American foreign policy – but a revolution of their own making, for their

own welfare, and for the security of freedom everywhere. The
Communists offer them another kind of revolution, glittering
and seductive in its superficial appeal. The choice between
the two can be made only by the Vietnamese people them-
selves. But in these times of trial and burden, true friendships
stand out. As Premier Diem recently wrote a great friend of
Vietnam, Senator Mansfield, "It is only in winter that you
can tell which trees are evergreen." And I am confident that
if this nation demonstrates that it has not forgotten the people
of Vietnam, the people of Vietnam will demonstrate that they
have not forgotten us.

It was easier to move on from college than Vietnam. Many people understand college years, even those who do not attend. No one
understood Vietnam like those of us who were there and many of us
agreed that as a country we had let our Vietnamese friends down, but
there was nothing we could do about it. All we could do was get on
with our lives. For me that meant returning to New Jersey. Claire and
I were married on a cold but sunny day in January, 1975. January is
not a typical month for weddings but that fit our style. Staying focused
on a traditional path continues to be a challenge for me, but if anyone
can help me stay on track it is Claire. I was determined to make our life
together a happy one.

Today, April 30, 1975, Claire and I watched on T. V. the last chopper leaving the roof of the American Embassy in Saigon. Thousands of
Vietnamese breaking the iron gate of the Embassy grounds with suit-
cases, bundles of treasured possessions and children in tow were trying
desperately to leave before the Communists could wreak their revenge.
The Huey, the same type of chopper I had flown in and made countless
air assaults from, would only be able to carry a few fortunate souls to
the safety of the waiting aircraft carrier in the South China Sea.

Odysseus, after his twenty year adventure, returned home and
brought his ordeal to a satisfying conclusion by slaughtering those
suitors who had tormented his faithful wife Penelope, plotted the death
of his son Telemachus, abused his servants, and ate and drank freely
from the bounty of his kingdom. I feel discouraged and angry. The
journey so many of us took does not come to the same satisfying reso-

lution. So many men lost, so much time wasted, and treasure spent. I have a growing realization this will not be the last time a feckless congress or President will lead us into another hostility and settle for a less than complete victorious conclusion. Three million American men and women served in Vietnam and 500,000 saw combat of one form or another. Approximately 48,000 were killed in combat and another 10,000 died in non combat circumstances. What would the 150,000 seriously injured vets think about this betrayal and inaction by congress? I for one would never trust or vote for another Democrat again. DeGaulle's assessment in 1954, at least for the American congress rang true. Now we will see, as Max once lamented, what will happen to those "poor, dumb bastards if we lose this thing?".

APPENDIX A

Below are the actual 28 "Rules of Ranging" authored by Major Robert Rogers during the French and Indian War (1754-1763). The version used earlier in the book came from a novel by Kenneth Roberts, NORTH WEST PASSAGE. Roberts novel became a favorite movie of mine staring Spencer Tracy, Robert Young and Walter Brennan. I felt the fictional version better conveyed the mood I attempted to instill in the story with apologies to rangers, airborne or not, everywhere.

Mike Konz

Robert Rogers' 28 "Rules of Ranging" (Wikipedia)

1.   All Rangers are to be subject to the rules and articles of war; to appear at roll call every evening, on their own parade, equipped, each with a Firelock, sixty rounds of powder and ball, and a hatchet, at which time an officer from each company is to inspect the same, to see they are in order, so as to be ready on any emergency to march at a minute's warning; and before they are dismissed, the necessary guards are to be draughted, and scouts for the next day appointed.

2.   Whenever you are ordered out to the enemies forts or frontiers for discoveries, if your number be small, march in single file, keeping at such a distance from each other as to prevent one shot from killing two men, sending one man, or more, forward, and the like on each side, at the distance of twenty yards from the main body, if the ground you march over will admit of it, to give the signal to the officer of the approach of an enemy, and of their number, &c.

3.   If you march over marshes or soft ground, change your position,

and march abreast of each other to prevent the enemy from tracking you (as they would do if you marched in a single file) till you get over such ground, and then resume your former order, and march till it is quite dark before you encamp, which do, if possible, on a piece of ground which that may afford your sentries the advantage of seeing or hearing the enemy some considerable distance, keeping one half of your whole party awake alternately through the night.

4. Some time before you come to the place you would reconnoitre, make a stand, and send one or two men in whom you con confide, to look out the best ground for making your observations.

5. If you have good fortune to take any prisoners, keep them separate, till they are examined, and in your return take a different route from that I which you went out, that you may the better discover any party in your rear, and have an opportunity, if their strength be superior to yours, to alter your course, or disperse, as circumstances may require.

6. If you march in a large body of three or four hundred, with a design to attack the enemy, divide your party into three columns, each headed by a proper officer, and let those columns march in single files to the right and left keeping at twenty yards distance or more from that of the center, if the ground will admit, and let proper guards be kept in the front and rear, and suitable flanking parties at a due distance as before directed, with orders to halt on all eminences, to take a view of the surrounding ground, to prevent your being ambuscaded, and to notify the approach or retreat of the enemy, that proper dispositions may be made for attacking, defending, &c. And if the enemy approach in your front on level ground, form a front of your three columns or main body with the advanced guard, keeping out your flanking parties, as if you were marching under the command of trusty officers, to prevent the enemy from pressing hard on either of your wings, or surrounding you, which is the usual method of the savages, if their number will admit of it, and be careful likewise to support and strengthen your rear-guard.

7. If you are obliged to receive the enemy's fire, fall, or squat down, till it is over; but if superior, be careful to support and strengthen

your flanking parties, to make them equal to theirs, that if possible you may repulse them to your main body, in which case push upon them with the greatest resolution with equal force in each flank in center, observing to keep at a due distance from each other, and advance from tree to tree, with one half of the party before the other ten or twelve yards. If the enemy push upon you, let your front fire and fall down, and then let your rear advance thro' them and do the like, by which time those who before were in front will be ready to discharge again, and repeat the same alternately, as occasion shall require; by this means you will keep up such a constant fire, that the enemy will not be able easily to break your order, or gain your ground.

8. If you oblige your enemy to retreat, be careful, in your pursuit of them, to keep out your flanking parties, and prevent them from gaining eminences, or rising grounds, in which case they would perhaps be able to rally and repulse you in their turn.

9. If you are obliged to retreat, let the front of your whole party fire and fall back, till the rear bath done the same, making for the best ground you can, by this means you will oblige the enemy to pursue you, if you do it at all, in the face of a constant fire.

10. If the enemy is so superior that you are in danger if being sur-rounded by them, let the whole body disperse, and every one take a different road to the place of rendezvous appointed for that evening ensuing, in order to bring the whole party, or as many of them as possible, together, after any separation that may happen in the day; but if you should happen to be actually surrounded, form yourselves into a square, or if in the woods, a circle is best, and, if possible, make a stand till the darkness of the night favours your escape.

11. If your rear is attacked, the main body and flankers must face about to the right or left, as occasion shall require, and form them-selves to oppose the enemy, as before directed; and the same meth-od must be observed, if attacked in either of your flanks, by which means you will always make a rear of one of your flank-guards.

12. If you determine to rally after a retreat, in order to make a fresh stand against the enemy, by all means endeavour to do it on the

most rising ground you come at, which will give you greatly the advantage in point of situation, and enable you to repulse superior numbers.

13. In general, when pushed upon by the enemy, reserve your fire till they approach very near, which will give you an opportunity of rushing upon them with your hatchets and cutlasses to the better advantage

14. When you encamp at night, fix your sentries in such a manner as not to be relieved from the main body till morning, profound secrecy and silence being often of the last importance in these cases. Each sentry therefore should consist of six men, two of whom must be constantly alert, and when relieved by their fellows, it should be done without noise; and in case those on duty see or hear anything, which alarms them, they are not to speak, but one of them is silently to retreat, and acquaint the commanding officer thereof, that proper dispositions may be made; and all occasional sentries should be fixed in like manner.

15. At the first dawn of day, awake your whole detachment; that being the time when the savages choose to fall upon their enemies, you should by all means be in readiness to receive them.

16. If the enemy should be discovered by your detachments in the morning, and their numbers are superior to yours, and a victory doubtful, you should attack them till the evening, as then they will not know your numbers, and if you are repulsed, your retreat will be favoured by the darkness of the night.

17. Before you leave your encampment, send out small parties to scout round it, to see if there be any appearance or track of an enemy that might have been near you during the night.

18. When you stop for refreshment, choose some spring or rivulet if you can, and dispose your party so as not to be surprised, posting proper guards and sentries at a due distance, and let a small party waylay the path you came in, lest the enemy should be pursuing.

19. If, in your return, you have to cross rivers, avoid the usual fords as much as possible, lest the enemy should have discovered, and be

there expecting you.

20. If you have to pass by lakes, keep at some distance from the edge of the water, lest, in case of an ambuscade or an attack from the enemy, when in the situation, your retreat should be cut off.

21. If the enemy pursue your rear, take a circle till you come to your own tracks, and there form an ambush to receive them, and give them the first fire.

22. When you return from a scout, and come near our forts, avoid the usual roads, and avenues thereto, lest the enemy should have headed you, and lay in ambush to receive you, when almost exhausted with fatigues.

23. When you pursue any party that has been near our forts or encampments, follow not directly in their tracks, lest they should be discovered by their rear guards, who, at such time, would be most alert; but endeavour, by a different route, to head and meet them in some narrow pass, or lay in ambush to receive them when and where they least expect it.

24. If you are to embark in canoes, battoes, or otherwise, by water, choose the evening for the time of your embarkation, as you will then have the whole night before you, to pass undiscovered by any parties of the enemy, on hills, or other places, which command a prospect of the lake of river you are upon.

25. In paddling or rowing, give orders that the boat or canoe next the sternmost, wait for her, and the third for the second, and the fourth for the third, and so on, to prevent separation, and that you may be ready to assist each other on any emergency.

26. Appoint one man in each boat to look out for fires, on the adjacent shores, from the numbers and size of which you may form some judgment of the number that kindled them, and whether you are able to attack them or not.

27. If you find the enemy encamped near the banks of a river or lake, which you imagine they will attempt to cross for their security upon being attacked, leave a detachment of your party on the oppo-

site shore to receive them, while, with the remainder, you surprise them, having them between you and the lake or river.

28. If you cannot satisfy yourself as to the enemy's number and strength, from their fire, &c. conceal your boats at some distance, and ascertain their number by a reconnoitering party, when they embark, or march, in the morning, marking the course they steer, &c. when you may pursue, ambush, and attack them, or let them pass, as prudence shall direct you. In general, however, that you may not be discovered by the enemy upon the lakes and rivers at a great distance, it is safest to lay by, with your boats and party concealed all day, without noise or shew; and to pursue your intended route by night; and whether you go by land or water, give out parole and countersigns, in order to know one another in the dark, and likewise appoint a station every man to repair to, in case of any accident that may separate you.

APPENDIX B

ABBREVIATIONS & TERMS

AK 47   Automatic Rifle – Avtomat Kalashnikova – Russian Soviet Army's weapon of choice. Developed by Mikhail Kalashnikov in 1945 final version developed in 1947.

ARVN   Army of the Republic of Vietnam

AWOL   Absent Without Leave

Boonies   Boondocks, jungle, area away from base camp

Chopper   Helicopter

C.O.   Commanding Officer

D. I.   Drill Instructor

D. Z.   Drop Zone – landing area for paratroopers

Fire Base   Camp for artillery units in boonies – usually on top of a hill

F. O.   Forward Observer

Grunt   Nickname for infantry troops both airborne and legs

Klick   1000 meters = 1093 yards

Leg	Non-airborne infantry men
L. Z.	Landing Zone - for helicopters
L.R.R.P	Long Range Reconnaissance Patrol
N. C. O	Non Commissioned Officer (Sergeant)
NVA	North Vietnamese Army
Pickett's Charge	At the Battle of Gettysburg Major General George Pickett of the Confederate Army led the last assault of the Union line on Cemetery Ridge across an open field approximately 1700 yards wide with 12,500 men resulting in the devastation of his force of nine brigades. In the opinion of many historians and military experts this was a foolish and unnecessary attack.
Poncho	Rain gear – also used for makeshift tent when in the boonies
Poncho Liner	Used as a blanket in the boonies – made of synthetic fiber to deflect dampness
R. A.	Regular Army (volunteers)
R T. O.	Radio Telephone Operator
V. C.	Viet Cong
Viet Cong	South Vietnamese Communist
Viet Minh	Name of Vietnamese Communists during the French-Indochina War -short for League for the Independence of Vietnam

ABOUT THE AUTHOR

Mike Konz was a Sergeant with the 1ˢᵗ Cavalry and the 82ⁿᵈ Airborne in Vietnam. Having grown up in New Jersey, Mike now resides in eastern Pennsylvania with his wife of 40 years. Kay and Mike, who have four adult children, have owned and operated several restaurants and other small businesses.

CPSIA information can be obtained at www.ICGtesting.com
Printed in the USA
LVOW06s1757260214

375274LV00003B/635/P